loveactually

loveactually

Richard Curtis

Screenplay edited by Emma Freud

Photographs by Peter Mountain

MICHAEL JOSEPH
an imprint of
PENGUIN BOOKS

MICHAEL JOSEPH

Published by the Penguin Group
Penguin Books Ltd, 80 Strand, London WC2R 0RL, England
Penguin Group (USA), Inc., 375 Hudson Street, New York, New York 10014, USA
Penguin Books Australia Ltd, 250 Camberwell Road, Camberwell, Victoria 3124, Australia
Penguin Books Canada Ltd, 10 Alcorn Avenue, Toronto, Ontario, Canada M4V 3B2
Penguin Books India (P) Ltd, 11 Community Centre, Panchsheel Park, New Delhi – 110 017, India
Penguin Books (NZ) Ltd, Cnr Rosedale and Airborne Roads, Albany, Auckland, New Zealand
Penguin Books (South Africa) (Pty) Ltd, 24 Sturdee Avenue, Rosebank 2196, South Africa

Penguin Books Ltd, Registered Offices: 80 Strand, London WC2R 0RL, England

www.penguin.com

First published 2003
1

This book is dedicated to my darling sister Belinda –
and to all the people we filmed at Heathrow who spontaneously
said 'yes' and are now caught on film kissing for ever.

love actually from Neely
and Bowen Atkinson.

Contents

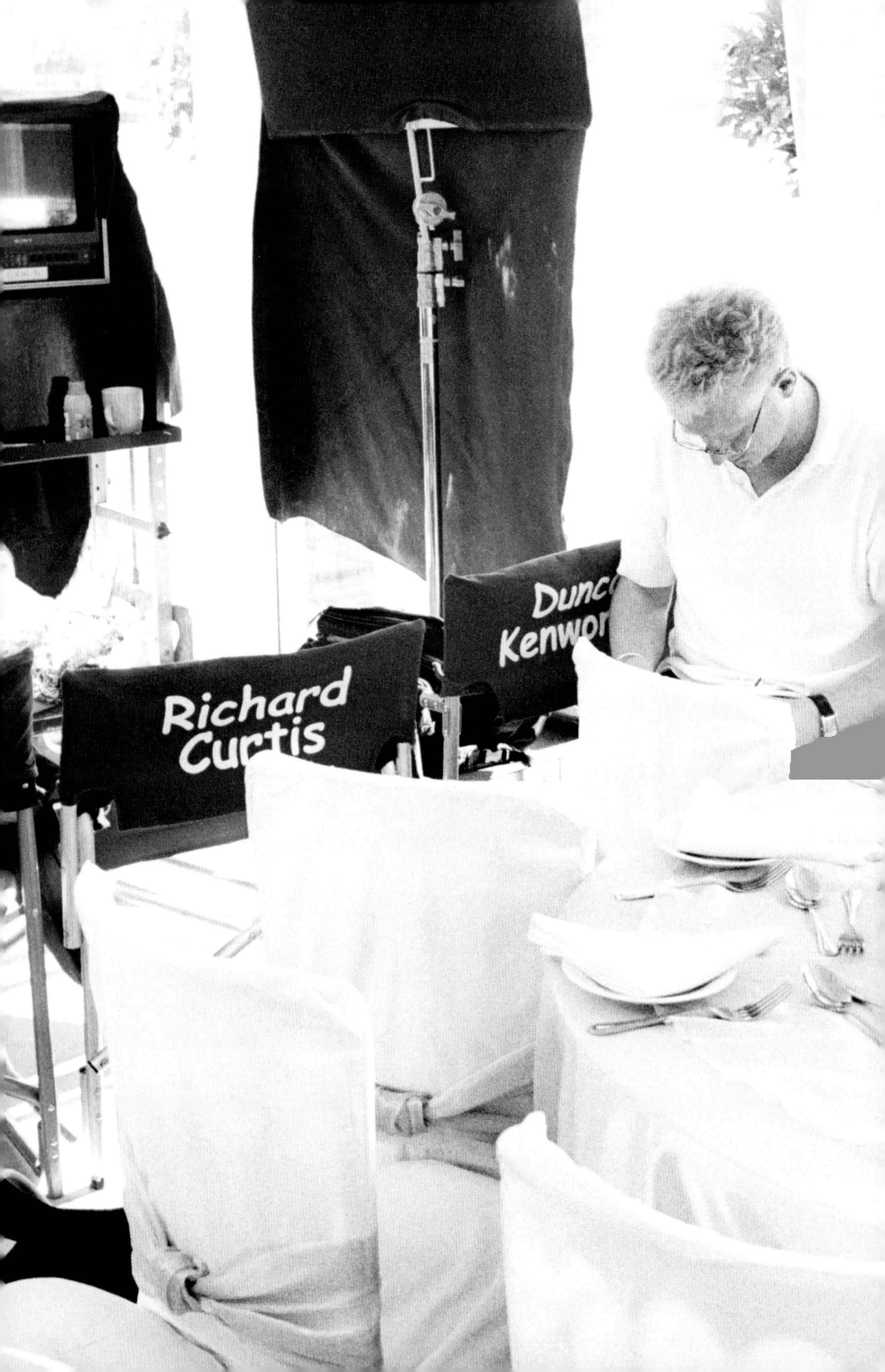
Richard
Curtis

Introduction
by Richard Curtis

'I was scared, I was scared, tired and underprepared ...'

I used to hum that Coldplay song to myself every morning as I got up to direct the film of which this is the book. It was a tiny bit of comfort to know that Chris Martin, a man who's dated Gwyneth Paltrow, had once been through as bad a time as me.

But fortunately – this isn't the place to write about the difficulties of directing ... though just for the record the five that spring to mind are:

1. It is impossible to resist the bacon sandwich that you are offered when you get to the set at 7.00 am. It is then impossible to refuse the next one you are offered two hours later at 9.00 am, because after all it is still easily breakfast time. And then the bastards slip you one at 11.15 am. This means that all directors put on weight during the shoot (see Hitchcock, Coppola, Peter Jackson – all the best guys are chubby), which means that the whole point of directing – to become attractive enough to go out with someone like Gwyneth Paltrow is defeated by the fact that by the time you finish the film you've become a great big Shrek-sized chubster no film star would look at twice.

2. You have to actually finish stuff every day. The great thing about writing is that you can always rewrite the next day – but directing you've just got the one day and then you move on. Writers have it very easy. I see that now.

3. Everybody keeps asking you questions – which is great if you know the answers, but not so good if you're a first-time director and don't know anything. I was disappointed that my catchphrase on the shoot became 'I don't know – do you?'

4. You have to remember to say 'action'. This is really hard. Everything is all set up, the actors are in place and then it all goes quiet. You sit there saying to yourself, 'Come on, come on, actors – act – everything's all set up.' But they seem frozen – lost in a world of weird stillness. And then you remember that you are the director and you say 'action' and at last it all begins.

And if you're lucky it goes well – and the actors act it right and the camera moves right and you're thrilled – and so you get up and help yourself to another bacon sandwich, and wander round, pleased . . . until you realize that you're entirely alone and everyone else is still on set, improvising in a rather weird way – and then you remember that you are the director and you're also meant to say 'cut'. And that's the fifth difficult thing . . .

5.   You have to remember to say 'cut'.

But, as I say – this is not the place to talk about directing – this is the place to say something about writing a screenplay such as this one. So here, for the record, are the five stages in writing the script of *Love Actually*.

1.   It all started exactly twenty-eight years ago when I first saw *Nashville* by Robert Altman (if you haven't seen it, see it now – it still seems perfect to me). It immediately became my favourite film. Then a few years ago I realized that a lot of films I've loved recently – *Pulp Fiction, Short Cuts*, Wayne Wang's perfect *Smoke* and a whole series of Woody Allen films, such as *Hannah and Her Sisters* and the great *Crimes and Misdemeanours* – are all films with lots of plots. And I thought that I'd like to have a go at writing that kind of film – to see if it was possible to write a film with nine beginnings, nine snappy middles and nine ends – without any of the stuff in between.

2.   It all began again while I was away in Bali for six months in 2000. I'd had a back operation and had to go for a long walk every day – and I tried to think up a new

story each time I walked. The stories in the film are all stories I thought of then – although a couple I'd thought of before and just thought in Bali that they might fit into the film. The strange thing is that, think as hard as I might, I never managed to think of any stories about Bali at all. It is a tragic truth that my imagination seems to stop at the Hammersmith Flyover.

3. I then returned to England and started to write the film. At one point it was five hours long – and my girlfriend, Emma, who edits all my scripts, aged a good five years during the reading of it. Amongst the stories that she cut were the one about the gay schoolgirls, the one about the Lucian Freud pictures discovered in a beach-hut, the one about my friend Howard and the unfortunate incident in the recording studio, the one about the man who meets Debbie Harry on the subway – and the one about the time my friend Helen Fielding actually fell asleep while out on a date with me – I had to finish my dinner, in a crowded restaurant, while she sat with her face flat on the table, snoring gently.

4. When the script got down to about two and a half hours we thought it was okay and handed it in to our producers. We then had a read-through with some fantastic actors and realized it wasn't okay at all and changed it again. Then we had another read-through with the full cast (the pictures of this are below) and then we changed it a bit again. Then we shot the film – and it went back up again to three and a half hours. Not only that – three and a half hours in totally the wrong order with no jokes. That first viewing was not a good day. Then we started to edit.

5. So this script you're about to read is living proof that a film isn't written once, it's written at least three times – first it's written, then it's rewritten as you direct it and then it's rewritten as you edit it.

I hope you enjoy the book – and just to give you something to think about when you get to the dull bits, here are five other little things you might be interested in if you like the film.

1. The lake in which we shot Colin Firth and Lucia Moniz was 18 inches deep. They're kneeling and pretending to swim. In the rushes, at the end of every take you can see them stand up and the water only comes up to their knees. During the filming, Colin was bitten by a vicious, malarial gadfly – his elbow swelled up like an avocado and, were he not a saint, he would have sued us for the entire profits of the film.

2. Helder Costa, who plays Aurelia's father, is probably Portugal's greatest theatre director. It's like having Trevor Nunn or Stephen Daldry playing a bit part in your film. Unfortunately, no one told me this – so I spent the two days we were working together giving him really pathetic notes, and acting out how I wanted it to be and saying 'Louder, louder!' and 'Come on! Be better, better.' And then the morning before he left he came downstairs and gave me a 400-page coffee-table book about his life, work and theatre company. So look at him with respect, even though I made him wear a string vest.

3. Sticking to the Portuguese plot – I think it's important for people to realize that Lucia represented Portugal in the Eurovision Song Contest in 1996. The fact that she came sixth is only further proof of how insanely unreliable the voting system of the contest is. If you press her, she agrees she should have come eighth.

4. In Hugh Grant's first scene, we did the long shot when he arrives at Downing Street before lunch, and the close-ups of him and Martine after lunch. During lunch he took a rest. When he woke up, he put on the wrong tie. And no one noticed. So if you look carefully, the Prime Minister swaps ties eleven times during the scene.

5. Billy Bob Thornton was unusual – he took the part without actually reading the script, because he liked the letter we wrote him. The first day on the set I asked him where he was staying. He told me the name of the hotel, then added that, as I probably knew, there weren't all that many hotels he could stay in in London. I said I didn't know that – why? He replied that he had a problem with antique furniture and was uncomfortable being in the same room as it. We were standing in the set of Downing Street and I asked him if he was okay with the furniture in the room. He replied, 'Yes – but there are a couple of pieces in the next room I'm a little frightened of.'

RC: Wow. Any other strange phobias I should know about?

BBT: Not really – well, maybe just the one.

RC: Tell me.

BBT: I have a real problem with Benjamin Disraeli.

RC: Benjamin Disraeli – the nineteenth-century British Prime Minister?

BBT: Well, no – not actually Benjamin Disraeli. Who could be frightened by Benjamin Disraeli? More Benjamin Disraeli's facial hair – I can't bear to be anywhere near that man's moustache – or beard for that matter. Or any representation of it.

It was at that point I felt bound to inform him that the next scene was set on the PM's staircase, which has portraits of all former British Prime Ministers on it, including – this must have been a million-to-one chance – a portrait of Benjamin Disraeli. And his beard. And his moustache. Billy turned white. But he is a true professional and went through the next day uncomplaining. However, you will notice if you watch the film carefully, he never glances up the staircase for fear of his life.

Now I've typed this out I'm starting to ask myself – was he taking the mickey out of me? I'm worried now – he said it with a very straight face, but then he's a very good actor. I just don't know. What I do know is that he made up the line 'That's a pretty little sonofabitch right there – did you see those pipes?' The line I wrote was something like 'Wow – she's pretty, isn't she.' But then Bob's a genius – and I ain't.

What follows is the proof of that pudding.

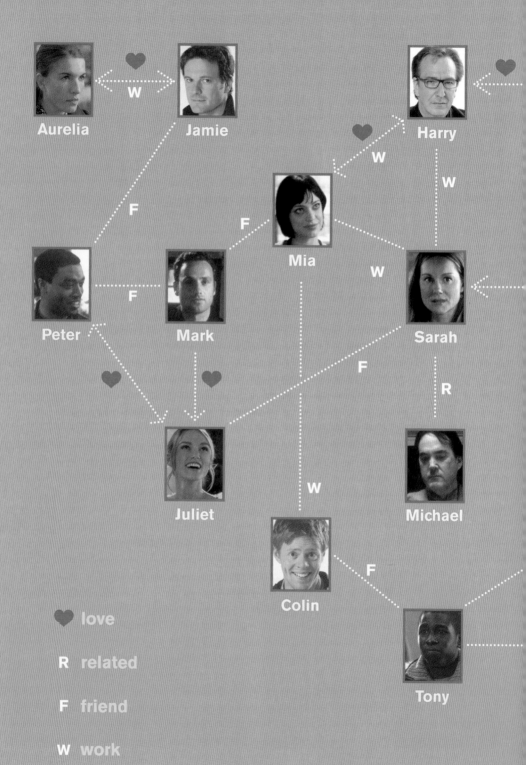

Aurelia ♥ **W** → **Jamie**

Harry ♥

♥ **W** **Mia**

Harry **W**

F (Jamie to Peter)

Peter **F** **Mark**

F (Mia) **W** **Sarah**

W

F (Sarah)

R

♥ **Peter** ♥ **Mark**

Juliet

Michael

W (Mia to Colin)

Colin

F **Tony**

♥ **love**

R **related**

F **friend**

W **work**

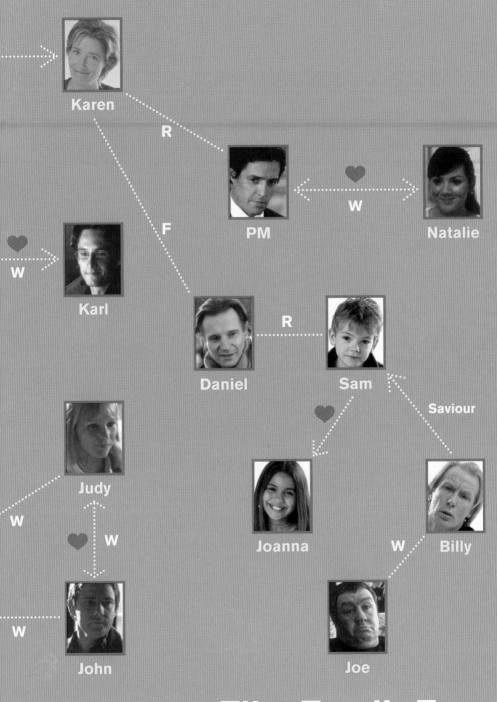

Karen

R

F

PM

W

Natalie

W

Karl

Daniel

R

Sam

Saviour

Judy

Joanna

Billy

W

W

W

John

W

Joe

Film Family Tree

Love Actually
The Screenplay

1 INT. HEATHROW AIRPORT – ARRIVALS GATE. DAY.

Darkness – then real documentary footage of the most miscellaneous of groups and couples at the arrivals gate, all kissing, all full of affection and emotion. A voice over begins.

PM (v/o): Whenever I get gloomy with the state of the world, I think about the Arrivals Gate at Heathrow Airport. General opinion's starting to make out that we live in a world of hatred and greed – but I don't see that. Seems to me that love is everywhere. Often it's not particularly dignified, or newsworthy – but it's always there – fathers and sons, mothers and daughters, husbands and wives, boyfriends, girlfriends, old friends. Before the planes hit the Twin Towers, as far as I know, none of the phone calls from the people on board were messages of hate and revenge – they were all messages of love. If you look for it, I've got a sneaking suspicion you'll find that love actually is all around …

2 INT. RECORDING STUDIO. NIGHT.

Cut to a recording studio – a wonderful looking, battered 55-year-old ex-giant of rock is singing. Three noisy backing singers are really going for it beside him.

BILLY THE OLD ROCKER:
'I feel it in my fingers,
I feel it in my toes.
Love is all around me – and so the …'

Joe, his manager, is in the control room with the engineer. Joe is unprepossessing, woolly, chubby, moist, in his forties.

JOE: I'm afraid you did it again, Bill.

BILLY: It's just I know the old version so well, you know.

JOE: Well, we all do – that's why we're making the new version.

BILLY: Right. Okay – let's go.

The intro strikes up again …

BILLY:
'I feel it in my fingers,
I feel it in my toes.
Love is all…'
Oh fuckwankbuggershittingarseheadandhole.
Start again…(*the intro plays*)
'I feel it in my fingers,
I feel it in my toes.
Christmas is all around me…'

Cut to Joe – deeply pleased.

'And so the feeling grows.
It's written in the wind,
It's everywhere I go.
So if you really love Christmas,
Come on and let it snow…'
(*to Joe*) This is shit, isn't it?

JOE: Yup – solid gold shit, Maestro.

3 EXT. VARIOUS LONDON SITES. DAY.

*Christmas trees being put up, London streets decorated with twinkling Christmas
lights, ice skaters whirling round the ice rink at Somerset House … the city is glowing
as the build up to Christmas begins.*

4 INT. JAMIE'S HOUSE. DAY.

*Cut to Jamie. Thirty-eight, good-looking and good-natured. Preparing to go out but
running late. His girlfriend Katya, who is curled up sick in bed, watches on. He speaks
with a slight, touching, mid-sentence stutter.*

JAMIE: God, I am so late.

KATYA: It's just round the corner, you'll make it.

JAMIE: You're sure you d-d-don't mind me going without you?

KATYA: No, really – I'm just feeling so rotten.

JAMIE: I love you.

He kisses her.

KATYA: I know.

JAMIE: I love you even when you're sick and look disgusting.

He kisses her again.

KATYA: I know. Now go, or you will actually miss it.

JAMIE: Right.

He walks out to leave and Katya falls back on to the pillows. Jamie sticks his head round the door again.

JAMIE: Did I mention that I love you?

KATYA: Yes you did. Get out, loser!

Jamie leaves.

5 INT. DANIEL'S HOUSE. DAY.

Daniel, a recent widower, sits very alone in his office in his house, his head in his hands. A moment of stillness and sorrow. Then he lifts his head, picks up the phone and dials …

DANIEL: Karen? It's me again. Sorry, I literally don't have anyone else to talk to.

Karen is in her kitchen – obviously mid-forties, very English, still quite nice-looking, and good.

KAREN: Absolutely. Horrible moment right now though – can I call back?

DANIEL: Of course.

KAREN: Doesn't mean I'm not terribly concerned that your wife just died.

DANIEL: Understood. Bugger off and call me later.

He hangs up.

6 INT. KAREN'S HOUSE. DAY.

Karen goes back to the question in hand. She turns to her daughter, Daisy, who is sweet and seven.

KAREN: So – what's this big news then?

DAISY: We've been given our parts in the Nativity play. And I'm the lobster.

KAREN: The lobster?

DAISY: Yes.

KAREN: In the Nativity play?

DAISY: Yes. First Lobster.

KAREN: There was more than one lobster present at the birth of Jesus?

DAISY: Durr...

7 EXT. FAIRTRADE OFFICE. DAY.

Colin's van pulls up outside the Fairtrade office – he steps out of it.

8 INT. FAIRTRADE OFFICE. DAY.

Colin enters – he's the guy who brings sandwiches round to companies. It's an interesting place – a mixture between a charity and the Body Shop – big and messy – fifty people – lots of smartly designed posters and marketing stuff on desks and walls. Colin is very bouncy and chatty.

COLIN: Best sandwiches in Britain.

He throws a sandwich on to someone's desk.

COLIN: Try my lovely nuts.

He hands a girl a packet, beaming at her.

COLIN: Beautiful muffin for a beautiful lady.

Another uninterested girl gets a muffin she didn't ask for.

COLIN: Morning, my future wife.

He smiles at a beautiful girl at one desk – no reaction. Stay with her – her name is Mia. She gets up and goes to knock on the door behind her.

9 INT. FILM STUDIO. DAY.

Cut to a couple having slightly weird sex rather half-heartedly. They're both dressed, and he appears to be taking her from behind. She is leaning forward against a pillar in a stylish, dramatically lit bedroom, probably in Venice.

DIRECTOR OF PHOTOGRAPHY (v/o): Okay – you can stop there, thanks …

Cut back to show the paraphernalia of a film crew. The D.O.P. immediately slips into discussion with the director. The two stand-ins, because that's what they are, start to chat. They're two plain, sweet, simple people.

JOHN: By the way – he introduced me as John, but actually everyone calls me Jack.

JUDY: Oh fine – nice to meet you, Jack. He got me right though – I'm just Judy.

JOHN: Great, Just Judy.

10 INT. CHURCH. DAY.

Cut to two men's faces. They are dressed in wedding ties and coats. The best man and groom waiting at the end of an aisle. The church is sunny and full.

PETER: No surprises?

MARK: No surprises.

PETER: Not like the stag night?

MARK: Unlike the stag night.

PETER: Do you admit that the Brazilian prostitutes were a mistake?

MARK: I do.

PETER: And it would have been much better if they'd not turned out to be men?

MARK: That is true. Good luck, kiddo.

A manly Roman handshake. Mark picks up his video and starts discreetly to film proceedings – it's one of those cameras where you can view through a screen rather than holding it to your eye. Behind them the doors of the church open to let in a really lovely, optimistic girl in her wedding dress. This is Juliet.

11 EXT. 10 DOWNING STREET. DAY.

Cut to outside 10 Downing Street – huge noise – press and people. Out of a car steps the new Prime Minister. He waves – huge cheer. He's an attractive man in his forties.

He enters – the door closes behind him.

12 INT. 10 DOWNING STREET – ENTRANCE HALL. DAY.

Suddenly, silence and formality inside in comparison to the chaos outside.

There to greet him is his personal adviser, Annie. She is strong and intelligent-looking. His demeanour immediately changes, he deformalizes.

ANNIE: Welcome, Prime Minister.

PM: I must work on my wave. How are you?

He kisses her hello.

ANNIE: How are you feeling?

PM: Cool. Powerful.

ANNIE: Would you like to meet the household staff?

PM: Yes, I would like that very much indeed. Anything to put off actually running the country.

He heads with her towards a line of employees.

ANNIE: This is Terence. He's in charge.

TERENCE: Good morning, sir.

PM: Good morning. Had an uncle called Terence once – hated him – I think he was a pervert – but I very much like the look of you.

ANNIE: This is Pat.

PM: Hello, Pat.

PAT: Good morning, sir. I'm the Housekeeper.

PM: Oh, right. Should be a lot easier with me than with the last lot – no nappies, no teenagers, no scary wife.

ANNIE: And this is Natalie – she's new, like you.

PM: Hello, Natalie.

NATALIE: Hello, David – I mean 'sir'. Shit, I can't believe I just said that – and now I've gone and said 'shit' – twice. I'm so sorry, sir.

PM: That's fine … You could have said 'fuck' and then we'd have been in real trouble.

NATALIE: Thank you, sir. I did have an awful premonition I was going to fuck up on my first day … oh piss it!

He laughs. She blushes hugely – a lovely, young, bright-faced girl. He looks at her. Something's happening.

ANNIE: Right – I'll go get my things – and then let's fix the country, shall we?

PM: Yeah, I can't see why not.

As he walks away, he just casually looks back over his shoulder – Natalie is one of the things he looks back on.

13 INT.10 DOWNING STREET – PM'S OFFICE. DAY.

PM enters, and closes the door behind him.

PM: Oh no. That is so inconvenient.

14 INT. CHURCH. DAY.

VICAR: In the presence of God, Peter and Juliet have given their consent and made their marriage vows to each other. They declared their marriage by the giving and receiving of rings. I therefore proclaim that they are husband and wife.

Peter and Juliet kiss, and the congregation, including Jamie and Sarah, a sweet, smiling American woman in her thirties, erupt into applause. Peter turns.

PETER: And you resisted the temptation for any surprises?

MARK: Yes. I'm mature now.

Now bride and groom turn and head down the aisle. The organ strikes up a traditional church exit song. Then it suddenly stops. Peter and Juliet look a bit surprised.

As the music changes, a curtain that has been hiding the contents of the balcony drops. Behind it is a twenty-strong choir. They begin to sing 'All You Need Is Love'.

Juliet, is radiant – adoring it . . .

JULIET: Did you do this?

PETER: Er – no.

Peter looks at Mark. Mark shrugs his shoulders, pretending he had absolutely no idea this was going to happen. Then beside the organ upstairs emerges a fabulous-looking singer, standing at a microphone – he begins to sing.

They are now joined, during the chorus, magically from all over the church, by new instrumentalists – three trumpets, two flutes, three trombones and two saxophones. They actually appear in the pews where they've been hiding their instruments till now.

Then as the chorus ends, an electric guitarist is suddenly in the pulpit, playing magnificently for his life.

15 INT. JAMIE'S HOUSE. DAY.

Jamie speeds through the door into his living room. At that moment another slightly younger man enters the room from the kitchen.

JAMIE:　Hello. What the hell are you doing here?

CHRIS:　Oh, I just popped over to borrow some old CDs.

JAMIE:　The lady of the house let you in, did she?

CHRIS:　Yeah.

JAMIE:　Lovely o-o-obliging girl. Just thought I'd pop back before the reception, see if she was better. Listen, I've been thinking. I think perhaps we ought to take Mum out for her birthday on Friday, what do you think? I just feel we've been bad sons this year.

CHRIS:　Okay, sounds fine – a bit, you know, boring, but fine.

KATYA (V/O):　Hurry up big boy, I'm naked and I want you at least twice before Jamie gets home.

Jamie looks at Chris… Chris looks at Jamie. Not a great brotherly moment.

16 INT. RECEPTION HALL. DAY.

It's the river-side reception of the 'All You Need Is Love' wedding. The bride and groom are in the highest spirits.

The best man, Mark, is still filming. A perky waiter approaches him – it is Colin the sandwich man again.

COLIN:　Delicious delicacy?

MARK:　No thanks.

Colin heads on to Sarah, who is talking on her mobile.

COLIN:　Taste explosion?

She just shakes her head. Colin heads off discouraged but then sees a woman he likes the look of by the window. Instantly he is by her side.

COLIN:　Food?

NANCY:　No thanks.

COLIN: Yeah – bit dodgy, isn't it. Looks like a dead baby's finger. Oooh! – tastes like it too. I'm Colin, by the way.

NANCY: I'm Nancy.

COLIN: And what do you do, Nancy?

NANCY: I'm a cook.

COLIN: Ever do weddings?

NANCY: Yes, I do.

COLIN: They should have asked you to do this one.

NANCY: They did.

COLIN: God – I wish you hadn't turned it down.

NANCY: I didn't.

COLIN: Right.

17 INT. RECEPTION KITCHEN TENT. DAY.

Colin walks in with the canapé tray and sits down next to another quite geeky guy called Tony, a friend who's just come along for the ride. He wears normal clothes.

COLIN: I've just worked out why I can never find true love.

TONY: Why's that?

COLIN: It's English girls. They're stuck up, you see – and I'm primarily attractive to girls who are, you know, cooler, game for a laugh – like American girls. So I should just go to America – I'd get a girlfriend there instantly. What do you think?

TONY: I think it's crap, Colin.

COLIN: No, that's where you're wrong. American girls would seriously dig me with my cute British accent.

TONY: You don't have a cute British accent.

COLIN: Yes, I do, I'm going to America.

TONY: Colin – you're a lonely, ugly arsehole, and you must accept it.

COLIN: Never. I am Colin, God of Sex. I'm just on the wrong continent, that's all.

18 INT. FILM STUDIO. DAY.

JOHN: I thought I would never make it in today. The traffic was just . . .

JUDY: Oh, unbelievable.

The Assistant Director comes up. He is Tony, Colin's discouraging friend. He is not very comfortable with his job at this moment.

TONY: Judy – could you, ahm, take your top off this time – lighting and camera need to know when we're actually going to see the nipples and when we're not.

JUDY: Oh yes, okay, right. (*To John*) At least it's nice and warm in here.

JOHN: Absolutely. Isn't always the case. I was standing in for Brad Pitt once on *Seven Years in Tibet* – bloody freezing . . .

TONY: Sorry, guys, time's pretty tight and we have to get the actors in.

JUDY: Fine.

JOHN: I promise I won't look.

She laughs a bit, then takes her jumper and bra off – pulling a bit of a 'what can you do?' look at John. They start to mime the sex again. The cameraman stands very close, judging the light with his little machine.

TONY: And Jerry says, if you could just put your hands on her breasts . . .

JOHN: Oh, right, okay. (*To Judy*) Is that all right?

JUDY: Yes, yeah – fine.

JOHN: I'll warm them up.

He rubs his hands together as Judy laughs politely, before he cups her breasts.

TONY: And massage them, please.

JOHN: Right . . . It's Junction 13 that's just murder, isn't it – total gridlock this morning.

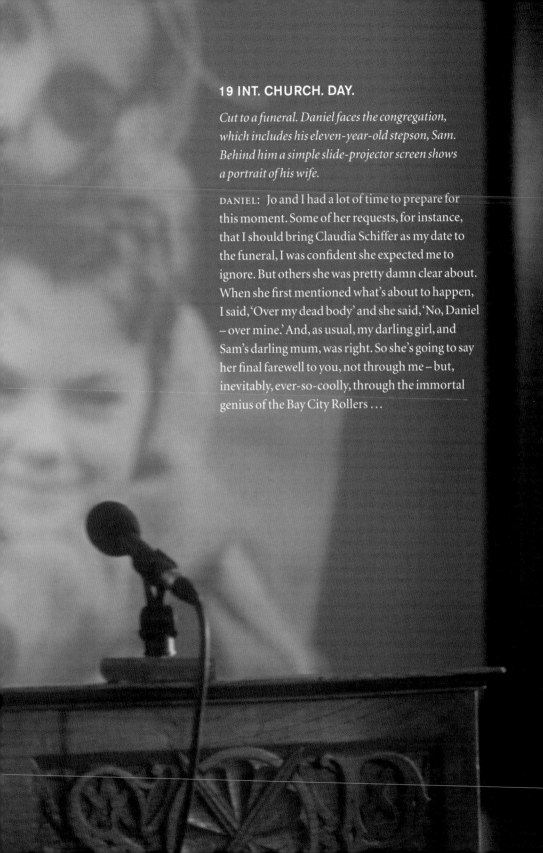

19 INT. CHURCH. DAY.

*Cut to a funeral. Daniel faces the congregation,
which includes his eleven-year-old stepson, Sam.
Behind him a simple slide-projector screen shows
a portrait of his wife.*

DANIEL: Jo and I had a lot of time to prepare for
this moment. Some of her requests, for instance,
that I should bring Claudia Schiffer as my date to
the funeral, I was confident she expected me to
ignore. But others she was pretty damn clear about.
When she first mentioned what's about to happen,
I said, 'Over my dead body' and she said, 'No, Daniel
– over mine.' And, as usual, my darling girl, and
Sam's darling mum, was right. So she's going to say
her final farewell to you, not through me – but,
inevitably, ever-so-coolly, through the immortal
genius of the Bay City Rollers . . .

Through the speakers wham the Bay City Rollers: the projector screen shows more shots of Jo, including an utterly gleeful twelve-year-old girl, clearly Jo, totally decked in the scarf, badges and hats of rollermania.

The congregation, which includes Sam's grandparents and Karen, are torn between smiles at the song and the stills, and the real sadness of it all. Four men, including Daniel, gather and lift the coffin.

20 INT. RECEPTION HALL. NIGHT.

Cut to the newlyweds dancing to 'Bye Bye Baby'. Mark is filming. Sarah comes and sits next to him. She looks at him curiously, then gently...

SARAH: Do you love him?

MARK: Who? What?

SARAH: No – I just thought I'd ask the blunt question, in case it was the right one and you needed someone to talk to about it and no one had ever asked you so you'd never been able to talk about it even though you might have wanted to...

MARK: No, no, 'no' is the answer. No. Absolutely not.

SARAH: So that's a 'no' then?

MARK: Yes. Ahm . . . this DJ . . . what d'you reckon – the worst in history?

SARAH: Probably. I think it all hangs on the next song.

Cut to the DJ . . .

DJ: Now here's one for the lovers. That's quite a few of you, I shouldn't be surprised and a half.

'Puppy Love' starts to play. The DJ is utterly absorbed in the moment.

MARK: He's done it. It's official.

SARAH: Worst DJ in the world.

21 INT. HARRY'S OFFICE. DAY.

Mia enters the office of Harry – in his mid-forties, stylish – quite a serious man – but with hidden places.

MIA: Sarah's waiting for you.

HARRY: Oh yes, of course, great – good, good. How you doing, Mia – you settling in fine – learning who to avoid?

MIA: Absolutely.

Sarah walks in as Mia leaves gracefully.

SARAH: Hi, Harry.

HARRY: Now, switch off your phone and tell me exactly how long it is that you've been working here?

SARAH: Two years, seven months, three days and I suppose, what – two hours.

HARRY: And how long have you been in love with Karl, our enigmatic chief designer?

Sarah is taken aback – she thought this was a total secret.

SARAH: Ahm – two years, seven months, three days and, I suppose, one hour and thirty minutes.

HARRY: I thought as much.

SARAH: Do you think everybody knows?

HARRY: Yes.

SARAH: Do you think Karl knows?

HARRY: Yes.

SARAH: Oh, that is bad news.

HARRY: And I just thought that maybe the time had come to do something about it …

SARAH: Like what?

HARRY: Invite him out for a drink – then after twenty minutes casually drop into the conversation the fact that you'd like to marry him and have lots of sex and babies.

SARAH: You know that?

HARRY: Yes. And so does Karl. Think about it. For all our sakes. It's Christmas.

SARAH: Certainly – excellent. Will do. Thanks, boss.

She opens the door to leave and a very good-looking guy walks in.

KARL: Hi, Sarah.

SARAH: (*totally casually*) Hi, Karl.

And she walks out.

22 INT. THE FAIRTRADE OFFICE. DAY.

We follow Sarah through the door. Her phone rings immediately. She answers.

SARAH: Babe, absolutely, fire away.

She turns to Mia at her desk.

Mia, could you turn that down? What is that?

We realise that in the background we have been listening to 'Christmas Is All Around'.

23 INT. RADIO STATION – STUDIO ONE. DAY.

A local radio station. DJ1 at the mic – 'Christmas Is All Around' is just coming to an end.

DJ1: And that was the Christmas effort by the once great Billy Mack – oh dear me – how are the mighty fallen. I can safely put my hand up my arse and say that's the worst record I've heard this century. Oh …

Looking through to the other side, DJ2 is frantically waving his arms and pointing at a copy of the schedule. DJ1 realizes his faux pas.

And coincidentally, I believe Billy is a guest on my friend Mike's show in a few minutes' time. Welcome back, Bill.

24 INT. RADIO STATION – FOYER. DAY.

Cut outside – Joe and Billy sitting there in the foyer, where the station's output is on. Not totally happy.

25 INT. RADIO STATION – STUDIO TWO. DAY.

Ten minutes later.

MIKE: So Billy – welcome back to the airwaves – new Christmas single – cover of 'Love Is All Around'.

BILLY: Except we've changed the word 'love' to 'Christmas'.

MIKE: Yes. Is that an important message to you, Bill?

BILLY: Not really, Mike – Christmas is a time for people with someone they love in their lives.

MIKE: And that's not you?

BILLY: That's not me, Michael – when I was young and successful, I was greedy and foolish and now I'm left with no one, wrinkled and alone.

MIKE: Wow. Thanks for that, Bill.

BILLY: For what?

MIKE: Well, for actually giving a real answer to a question. Doesn't often happen here at Radio Watford, I can tell you.

BILLY: Ask me anything you like – I'll tell you the truth.

MIKE: Best shag you ever had?

BILLY: Britney Spears – no, only kidding . . . She was rubbish.

MIKE: Okay – here's one – how do you think the new record compares to your old classic stuff?

BILLY: Come on, Mikey, you know as well as I do the record's crap. But . . .

Cut to Joe's very unhappy reaction.

. . . wouldn't it be great if Number One this Christmas wasn't some smug teenager but an old ex-heroin addict searching for a come-back at any price. All those young popsters, come Christmas Day, they'll be stretched out naked with a cute bird balancing on their balls and I'll be stuck in some dingy flat with my manager Joe – ugliest man in the world – fucking miserable because our fucking gamble didn't pay off. So if you believe in Father Christmas, children – like your Uncle Billy does – buy my festering turd of a record and particularly enjoy the incredible crassness of the moment when we try to squeeze an extra syllable into the fourth line . . .

MIKE: I think you're referring to 'If you really love Christmas'.

BILLY: 'Come on and let it snow.' Ouch.

MIKE: So here it is one more time – the dark horse for this year's Christmas Number One – 'Christmas Is All Around'. Thank you, Billy. After this, the news – is the new Prime Minister in trouble already?

Billy signals to Joe with a happy thumbs-up.

26 INT. 10 DOWNING STREET – CABINET ROOM. DAY.

All the Cabinet are there, sitting round that famous long table.

PM: Okay, what's next?

ALEX: The President's visit.

PM: Ah, yes, yes. I fear this is going to be a difficult one to play. Alex?

ALEX: There is a very strong feeling in the Party that we mustn't allow ourselves to be bullied from pillar to post like the last government.

JEREMY: Here, here. This is our first really important test. Let's take a stand.

PM: Right. Right. I understand that. But I have decided . . . not to. Not this time.

Big sigh . . .

We will of course try to be clever, but let's not forget America is the most powerful country in the world. I'm not going to act like a petulant child.

General grudging acceptance.

PM: Right – now who do you have
to screw around here to get a cup of
tea and a chocolate biscuit?

*At which moment Natalie enters with
refreshments. She looks up and smiles.*

(*abashed*) Right.

27 INT. 10 DOWNING STREET – PM'S OFFICE. DAY.

A knock on the door.

PM: Yup – come in.

It is Natalie, carrying some files and a tray…

NATALIE: These have just come through from the Treasury – and these are for you.

He smiles. The tray has a tea cup – with three biscuits on a plate.

PM: Excellent. Thanks a lot.

NATALIE: I was hoping you'd win – not that I wouldn't have been nice to the other bloke too. Just always given him the boring biscuits with no chocolate.

PM: Ha! Thanks very much, thanks … Natalie.

She leaves – he drops his head, slamming it on the table in despair.

Oh God. Come on, get a grip – you're the Prime Minister, for God's sake.

28 INT. FILM STUDIO – GILDED BEDROOM. DAY.

The two stand-ins having sex again – on a bed – she is on top of him, both naked.

JOHN: So what do you reckon to our new Prime Minister then?

JUDY: Oh, I like him – can't understand why he's not married, though.

JOHN: Oh, you know the type – married to his job. Either that or gay as a picnic basket.

Tony comes forward nervously with instructions.

TONY: Judy, if you could just lower the nipples and cheat them a bit to the left.

JOHN: I have to say, Judy, this is a real pleasure. It's lovely to find someone I can actually chat to.

JUDY: Thank you. Ditto.

TONY: And the move again please, Judy.

They move at the same time and knock into each other.

BOTH: Oh God, sorry!

29 EXT. TONY'S STREET. DAY.

Colin and Tony are in Colin's sandwich van – it says 'The Munch Mob' on the side. Loud music plays.

30 INT. COLIN'S VAN. DAY.

COLIN: Exciting news!

TONY: What?

COLIN: I've bought a ticket to the States – I'm off in three weeks.

TONY: No!

COLIN: Yes! To a fantastic place called … Wisconsin.

TONY: No!

COLIN: YES! Wisconsin babes – here comes Sir Colin!

TONY: No, Col! There ARE a few babes in America, I grant you, but they're already going out with rich, attractive guys.

COLIN: Nah, Tone – you're just jealous. You know perfectly well that any bar anywhere in America contains ten girls more beautiful and more likely to have sex with me than the whole of the United Kingdom.

TONY: That is total bollocks. You've actually gone mad now.

COLIN: NO! I'm wise. Stateside, I'm Prince William … without the weird family.

TONY: No, Colin! Nooooo!

COLIN: Yes!

TONY: Nyet!

COLIN: Da!

TONY: Nein!

COLIN: Ja, darling!

31 INT. HARRY'S OFFICE. DAY.

Mia is there – she is, it must be said, looking gorgeous in a tight black dress.

HARRY: Right. The Christmas party. Not my favourite night of the year – and your unhappy job to organize.

MIA: Tell me.

HARRY: Basic really – find a venue – over-order on the drinks – bulk buy the guacamolé and advise the girls to avoid Kevin if they want their breasts unfondled.

MIA: Wives and family and stuff?

HARRY: Yes – I mean, not children – but wives and girlfriends, etc…oh Christ, you haven't got some horrible six-foot, tight-T-shirt-wearing boyfriend you'll be bringing, have you?

MIA: No…I'll just be hanging round the mistletoe, hoping to be kissed.

She looks at him hard. Suddenly real electricity in the room.

HARRY: Really. Right.

She walks out – he sort of shakes his head in a 'wake-up/what's going on?' way.

32 INT. DANIEL'S HOUSE. DAY.

Cut to Daniel and Karen entering Daniel's house.

DANIEL: He now spends all the time in his room – I mean, he'll be up there now.

KAREN: There's nothing unusual about that – my horrid son Bernard stays in his room all the time. Thank goodness.

DANIEL: No, but Karen, this is *all* the time…

The camera leaves them and tracks up the stairs towards Sam's bedroom door…

DANIEL: And I'm afraid that there's something really wrong, you know – I mean clearly it's about his mum, but Christ, he might be injecting heroin into his eyeballs for all I know.

KAREN: At the age of eleven?

DANIEL: Maybe not into his eyeballs, maybe just his veins.

33 INT. DANIEL'S HOUSE. DAY.

Daniel and Karen, standing in the kitchen.

DANIEL: The problem is, it was his mum who always used to talk to him and I don't know . . . the whole stepfather thing seems to suddenly somehow matter, like it never did before.

KAREN: Listen – it was always going to be a totally shit time. Just be patient – and maybe check the room for needles.

DANIEL: And then when he sometimes does come out, it's obvious he's been crying.

Suddenly a wave of sorrow hits him and he starts to cry. Karen just touches his shoulder.

It was such a ridiculous waste – and if it's now going to ruin Sam's life as well – I just don't know.

KAREN: Get a grip. People hate sissies. No one's ever going to shag you if you cry all the time.

DANIEL: Yeah. Absolutely. Helpful.

34 EXT. LONDON BENCH. DAY.

Daniel and Sam sit together looking out across the river. Eventually Daniel takes the plunge.

DANIEL: So, what's the problem, Sammy-o? Is it just Mum – or is it something else? Maybe … school? Are you being bullied? Or is it – something worse – can you give me any clues at all?

SAM: You really want to know?

DANIEL: I really want to know.

SAM: Even though you won't be able to do anything to help?

DANIEL: Even if that's the case.

SAM: Okay. Well, the truth is – actually – I'm in love.

DANIEL: Sorry?

SAM: I know I should be thinking about Mum all the time, and I am, but the truth is I'm in love and I was before she died and there's nothing I can do about it ...

DANIEL: Aren't you a bit young to be in love?

SAM: No.

DANIEL: Okay, right. Well, I'm a little relieved.

SAM: Why?

DANIEL: Well, because I thought it would be something worse ...

SAM: Worse than the total agony of being in love?

DANIEL: Ahm ... no – you're right, total agony.

35 INT. FAIRTRADE OFFICE. NIGHT.

It's late. Sarah is at her desk – she is putting on a bit of make-up furtively. Then suddenly Karl is walking from the far end of the long office towards her. She watches him – he reaches her desk near the door.

KARL: Night, Sarah.

SARAH: Night, Karl.

He leaves. She throws her hands in the air, exasperated. Her phone rings. She answers.

Yup, absolutely, free as a bird – fire away.

36 EXT./INT. FARMHOUSE IN FRANCE. DAY.

Cut to total darkness. Then windows start to open – on the living room of Jamie's chaotic but lovely French farmhouse. Jamie, with his suitcases deposited in the middle of the room, is opening the windows, some of which have little angel silhouettes cut in the wood.

Back inside, Jamie stands in front of a little desk. He sits down in front of an old-fashioned typewriter.

JAMIE: Alone again. Naturally.

37 INT. 10 DOWNING STREET – PM'S OFFICE. NIGHT.

Cut to later that night. The PM is showing out a Minister, as he opens the door to find Natalie about to knock.

PM: Natalie.

NATALIE: Sir.

She enters with a pile of papers and files. Puts them down, and heads off. Then…

PM: Thanks, Natalie. I'm starting to feel uncomfortable about us working in such close proximity every day and me knowing so little about you. Seems… élitist and wrong.

NATALIE: Well, there's not much to know.

PM: Where do you live, for instance?

NATALIE: Wandsworth. The dodgy end.

PM: My sister lives in Wandsworth – so which exactly is the dodgy end?

NATALIE: Right at the end of the High Street – Harris Street – near the Queen's Head.

PM: Right, yes, that is dodgy. And you live with your … husband … boyfriend, three illegitimate but charming children?

NATALIE: No, I've just split up with my boyfriend actually, so I'm back with my Mum and Dad for a while.

PM: Oh, I'm sorry.

NATALIE: No, that's fine. I'm well shot of him … (*She pauses*) He said I was getting fat.

PM: I beg your pardon?

NATALIE: He says no one's going to fancy a girl with thighs the size of big tree trunks. Not a nice guy actually, in the end.

Suddenly there's a glimpse of vulnerability in her.

PM: Right … (*He appears to go back to work – then looks up casually*) You know, being Prime Minister, I could just have him murdered.

NATALIE: Thank you, sir – I'll think about it.

PM: Do – the SAS are absolutely charming – ruthless trained killers are just a phone call away.

They both look at each other and there's a little laugh. For a moment she was sad and he's cheered her up. She leaves.

Oh God. Did you have this kind of problem?

Cut up to a very stern portrait of Margaret Thatcher.

Of course you did, you saucy minx.

38 INT. DANIEL'S LIVING ROOM. NIGHT.

A bit later – Sam is sitting on the couch as Daniel paces round, full of energy.

DANIEL: We can definitely crack this. Remember I was a kid once too. Come on – it's someone at school – right?

SAM: Yup.

DANIEL: And what does she/he feel about you?

SAM: *She* doesn't even know my name. And even if she did, she'd despise me. She's the coolest girl in school and everyone worships her because she's heaven.

DANIEL: Good. Good. Well, basically . . . you're fucked, aren't you?

39 INT. TV STUDIO. DAY.

A CD:UK-type Saturday morning pop show. Ant and Dec and Billy are on air, standing next to a large display of prizes. Joe is watching on a monitor in the wings.

DEC: Hi there and welcome back. So, Billy – three weeks till Christmas and it looks like the real competition's going to be Blue.

BILLY: Yes, I saw them on the show last week. They weren't very nice about my record.

ANT: No. Little scamps!

BILLY: Yeah – but very, very talented musicians.

DEC: Billy, I understand you've got a prize for our competition winners?

BILLY: Yes, I have, Ant or Dec. It's a personalized felt-tip pen.

ANT: Oh great.

BILLY: It's brilliant. It even writes on glass. So if you've got a framed picture like, for instance, this one ... of Blue (*framed picture – a prize*) you can just write on it.

He draws a speech bubble above the band and then writes inside it 'we've got little pricks'.

DEC: Lot of kids watching, Billy.

BILLY: Oh yes. Hiya kids – here's an important message from your Uncle Bill: don't buy drugs – become a pop star, and they give you them for free.

ANT: And I do believe it's a commercial break. Thank goodness. We'll see you soon, bye!

Cut to Joe banging his head against the monitor.

40 INT. ART GALLERY/PETER'S OFFICE/JULIET'S OFFICE. DAY.

A modern photograph gallery. Mark is on the phone. Three schoolgirls giggle in the background, inspecting an enormous photo of four naked male bottoms.

MARK: (*to the girls*) Actually they're not funny – they're art. (*On the phone*) Okay – let's say Thursday, my place.

PETER: Great ...

Cut to Peter in his office, on the phone.

... but for now, I've got Juliet on the other line. Can I patch you through? She wants to ask you a favour.

Mark sighs. Not happy.

MARK: Okay – fine.

PETER: Thanks. And be nice.

MARK: I'm always nice.

PETER: You know what I mean, Marky. Be friendly.

MARK: I'm always ...

Funny clicking sound. Then ...

JULIET: Mark?

MARK: Hi. (*Dutifully*) How was the honeymoon?

JULIET: It was great. And thanks for the gorgeous send-off.

She is making the call from where she works. Pause.

MARK: So what can I do for you?

JULIET: It's only a tiny favour. I've just tried the wedding video and it's a complete disaster – it's come out all blue and wibbly.

MARK: I'm sorry.

JULIET: And I remember you filming a lot on the day – and I just wondered if I could look at your stuff.

MARK: Oh no – look – to be honest, I didn't really . . .

JULIET: Please. All I want is just one shot of me in a wedding dress that isn't bright turquoise.

MARK: Okay – I'll have a look – but to be honest I'm pretty sure I wiped it, so don't get any hopes up. Must go.

And the conversation is over. Juliet, as ever, is slightly taken aback by his unfriendliness.

41 INT. FAIRTRADE OFFICE. DAY.

Harry is with Sarah, who is sitting at her desk. We see a photo of a young man by her computer in the background.

HARRY: Any progress on our match-making plan?

SARAH: No. I've done fuck-all and never will because he's too good for me.

HARRY: How true.

Sarah smacks Harry, in mock annoyance. Harry smacks her back – then Sarah's mobile begins to ring.

HARRY: And of course, your mobile goes … (*Walking over to Mia*) So, how's the Christmas party going?

MIA: Good – think I've found a venue. Friend of mine works there.

HARRY: What's it like?

MIA: Good, good – it's an art gallery … full of dark corners for doing dark deeds.

She looks at him hard.

HARRY: Right, right. Good. Well, I suppose I should take a look at it, or something.

MIA: You should.

42 INT. FARMHOUSE IN FRANCE. DAY.

Cut to Jamie typing in France on an old-fashioned typewriter and paper. The doorbell rings. He leaves the desk.

43 INT./EXT. FARMHOUSE IN FRANCE – FRONT DOOR. DAY.

Jamie opens the door to a confident, middle-aged French woman, Eléonore. She is clearly in charge of the house in some way, with a nice thick French accent.

JAMIE: Bonjour, Eléonore.

ELÉONORE: Bonjour, Monsieur Bennett. Welcome back. And this year, you bring a lady guest?

JAMIE: Ah, no – change of situation. It's just me.

ELÉONORE: Ah. Am I sad, or not sad?

JAMIE: I think you're not surprised.

ELÉONORE: And you stay here till Christmas?

JAMIE: Yes.

ELÉONORE: Good. Well, I find you a perfect lady to clean the house. This is Aurelia.

The shot widens to reveal, standing back nervously, Aurelia – a pleasant enough looking dark-haired woman – about twenty-eight, wearing a very ordinary cheap dress under a red overcoat. Jamie moves out to greet her.

JAMIE: Bonjour, Aurelia.

AURELIA: (*very quietly*) Bonjour.

JAMIE: (*very bad accent*) Je suis t-t-très heureux de vous avoir ici.

She looks puzzled.

ELÉONORE: Unfortunately, she cannot speak French. Just like you. She is Portuguese.

JAMIE: Ah. Ahm . . . Ahm – bon giorno. Ahm – Eusebio . . . molto bueno.

He mimes a little bit of football.

ELÉONORE: I think she is ten years too young to remember there was a footballer called Eusebio – and 'molto bueno' is Spanish.

JAMIE: Right, right. Anyway, it's nice to meet you.

He moves back towards the house.

ELÉONORE: And perhaps you can drive her home at the end of her work.

JAMIE: Absolutely. Con grande plesoro.

ELÉONORE: Which is what? Turkish?

44 INT./EXT. JAMIE'S CAR IN FRANCE. DAY.

Aurelia and Jamie in the car. Total silence ... Jamie getting embarrassed.
He looks at the gorgeous valley they are driving through.

JAMIE: Bello ... bella.

She looks puzzled.

Montagno ... arbore.

She just looks slightly perplexed.

No, right. Silence is golden. As the Tremeloes said. Clever guys. Though I think
the original version was by Frankie Valli and the Four Seasons. G-g-great band.
'Ooooo-ooo-ooo' – oh shut up.

He just goes back to driving.

45 EXT. 10 DOWNING STREET. DAY.

Dramatic cut to huge crowds outside Downing Street – bright sunshine. Two large
official-looking cars accompanied by police sweep through the gates – and out of the first
one steps the American President. He is a glamorous, very charismatic man. The PM
and President shake hands at the door – these two are kings of their domains – but the
PM's style seems quieter, and more modest against the American's sexy confidence.

PM: Mr President, welcome.

46 INT. 10 DOWNING STREET – ENTRANCE HALL. DAY.

Cut inside the front door. There are lots of people – members of the Cabinet.

PM: Come on through. I'm sorry your wife couldn't make it by the way.

PRESIDENT: So is she – although she would have been kind of lonely, I'm sure ...

PM: Yes, pathetic, isn't it. Just never been able to tie a girl down. I'm not sure
politics and dating really go together.

PRESIDENT: Really? I never found that.

PM: Yes, well, the difference is that you're sickeningly handsome whereas
I look increasingly like my Aunt Mildred.

They walk up the stairs.

PM: I'm very jealous of your plane by the way

PRESIDENT: (*laughing*) Thank you. We love that thing, I'll tell you.

They pass Natalie.

PM: Ah, Natalie. Hi.

PRESIDENT: Morning, ma'am. How's your day so far?

Natalie acknowledges them with a smile and continues down the stairs.

Excellent … (*To the PM*) My goodness, that's a pretty little sonofabitch right there. Did you see those pipes?

PM: Yes, she's … terrific … at her job.

47 INT. 10 DOWNING STREET – SMALL MEETING ROOM. DAY.

A mixture of American and British officials sit round a table, including the PM and the President. The experts are talking. PM looking intently on. The meeting is very tense. It's clearly been going on for hours – lots of files and papers around.

AMERICAN EXPERT: No. Absolutely not. We cannot and will not consult on that either.

ALEX: That is unexpected.

PRESIDENT: Well, it shouldn't be. The last administration made it perfectly clear – we are just being consistent with their policies.

ALEX: But, with all respect, sir, they were bad policies.

The PM is clearly on Alex's side – but he is taking his promised moderating stance.

PM: Right – thanks, Alex – I don't think we're making progress here. Let's move on, shall we?

48 INT. 10 DOWNING STREET – PM'S OFFICE. NIGHT.

The PM flops down on the couch. It's the end of the day. The President is sitting opposite him.

PM: Well, now, that was an interesting day.

PRESIDENT: I'm sorry if our line was firm – there's no point tiptoeing around today and then just disappointing you for four years. I have plans – and I plan to see them through.

PM: Absolutely. Now, there's one final thing I think we should look at – very close to my heart – if you could just give me a second.

He gets up.

PRESIDENT: I'll give you anything you ask for – as long as it's not something I don't want to give.

PM walks out into the corridor – passing Natalie on the way with a tray of drinks. He waves at her in the awkward way of a man in love.

PM: Hi.

The camera continues to follow him.

Pathetic.

He goes into a second office, grabs a file and walks back towards his study. He enters – and something odd is going on. The President and Natalie are standing in a guilty proximity – his hand touching her hair. She blushes completely and moves a foot away.

The President is unthrown. Something weird happens to the sound for a second – this is awful for the PM.

PRESIDENT: Great Scotch.

NATALIE: I'll be going then.

She begins to walk out, her head bowed, past the PM.

PRESIDENT: Natalie – I hope to see much more of you, as our two great countries work toward a better future.

NATALIE: Thank you, sir.

She leaves.

The PM is clearly quite shaken by what's happened, but the President stares nonchalantly back at him. The PM's face starts to reveal a hardening determination. He's had a thought.

49 INT. 10 DOWNING STREET – CONFERENCE ROOM. DAY.

*Cut into the room of the final press conference. The PM and President
enter the room together and stand at lecterns ready to answer the
questions of the press. The PM looks very serious.*

PRESS PERSON: Mr President … has it been a good visit?

PRESIDENT: Very satisfactory indeed – we got what we came for
and our special relationship is still very special.

PRESS PERSON: Prime Minister?

Pause.

PM: I love that word 'relationship' – covers all manner of sins
doesn't it? I fear this has become 'a bad relationship' – a relationship
based on the President taking exactly what he wants – and casually
ignoring all those things that really matter to …

He looks up – through the crowd, at the back he spies Natalie.

… Britain. We may be a small country but we're a great one too.
A country of Shakespeare, Churchill, the Beatles, Sean Connery,
Harry Potter, David Beckham's right foot – David Beckham's left
foot, come to that. And a friend who bullies us is no longer a friend.
And since bullies only respond to strength – from now onward,
I will be prepared to be much stronger and the President should
be prepared for that.

*Huge excited photographing and writing from the press – this is
now a real story. At the back of the hall – or behind them – we see the
Cabinet members completely delighted, particularly Alex. At last
the PM has come off the fence. The press all shout out to get the
President's reaction.*

PRESS PEOPLE: Mr President! Mr President! Mr President …
what do you make of that?

*The PM looks across at him – the President looks back with a mixture
of anger and new-found respect.*

50 INT. 10 DOWNING STREET – PM'S OFFICE. NIGHT.

A cluster of people around the PM in his office. His Cabinet are very proud and over-excited. Enter PM's secretary.

PM'S SECRETARY: It's your sister on line four.

The PM picks up.

PM: Yes, I'm very busy and important, how can I help you?

51 INT. KAREN'S HOUSE. NIGHT.

Karen is on the phone.

KAREN: Have you gone completely insane?

PM: You can't be sensible all the time.

KAREN: You can if you're Prime Minister.

PM: Oh dear. It's the Chancellor of the Exchequer on the other line.

KAREN: No it isn't.

PM: I'll call you back.

KAREN: No you won't.

She hangs up and turns to her husband. It's Harry from the Fairtrade office.

The trouble with being the Prime Minister's sister is that it does put your life into rather harsh perspective. What did my brother do today? He stood up and fought for his country. And what did I do – I made a papier mâché lobster head.

HARRY: What is this we're listening to?

KAREN: Joni Mitchell.

HARRY: I can't believe you *still* listen to Joni Mitchell.

KAREN: I love her and true love lasts a lifetime. Joni Mitchell is the woman who taught your cold English wife how to feel.

HARRY: Did she? Oh well, that's good. I must write to her sometime and say thanks.

KAREN: Now which doll shall we give Daisy's little friend Emily – the one that looks like a transvestite, or the one that looks like a dominatrix?

52 INT. 10 DOWNING STREET – PM'S BEDROOM. NIGHT.

The PM very casual, very alone. He is getting ready for bed. The radio is switched on by his bedside.

RADIO VOICE: . . . it's almost enough to make you feel patriotic. So here's one for our arse-kicking Prime Minister. I think he'll enjoy this. A golden oldie for a golden oldie . . .

In kicks a cracking tune – 'Jump' by The Pointer Sisters.

At first the PM hardly reacts – but then as the song continues he begins to join in in little ways. He clearly really knows the song – its off-beats, its backing vocals. He starts to dance – it's been a good day.

53 INT. 10 DOWNING STREET – STAIRCASE. NIGHT.

The PM funks down the staircase.

54 INT. 10 DOWNING STREET – CORRIDOR. NIGHT.

The PM dances across the corridor – through one door, out another.

55 INT. 10 DOWNING STREET – BIG MEETING ROOM. NIGHT.

The PM is really rocking now. His secretary enters. For a moment he doesn't see her. Then he does.

PM: Yeah … ahm … Mary, I've been thinking. Can we move the Japanese ambassador to four o'clock tomorrow?

PM'S SECRETARY: Certainly, sir.

PM: Terrific. Thanks so much.

56 INT. FARMHOUSE IN FRANCE. DAY.

Jamie is eating breakfast. Aurelia enters – takes his coffee cup off the pile of papers.

JAMIE: Would you like the last, er …

He offers her a croissant. She smiles. (From now on when speech is in Portuguese, it's in italics.)

AURELIA: *Thank you very much – but no – if you saw my sister, you'd understand why.*

JAMIE: That's all right – more for me.

AURELIA: *Just don't go eating it yourself – you're getting chubbier every day.*

JAMIE: I'm lucky – I've got one of those constitutions where I never put on weight.

She looks at him and smiles. There's a friendship developing. The phone rings.
He picks up the telephone, thinking that is what is ringing.

JAMIE: Hello?

It's actually his mobile, which is still ringing. Laughing – they search for it, eventually
finding it in between the pages of a manuscript. Jamie finally answers.

Hello?

57 EXT. FARMHOUSE IN FRANCE – GARDEN. DAY.

Jamie is typing outside in a jumper, putting the finished papers under his coffee
cup – it's a lovely big ramshackle garden, with a lake. Aurelia comes with a fresh cup of
coffee and takes the old cup off the pile of papers, as she has done before.

JAMIE: Thank you.

But this time, because it's outside, moving the cup suddenly lets all the papers fly.
Aurelia leaps to grab them – and so does Jamie … But the pages are flying away –
and heading in the direction of the lake at the end of the garden.

AURELIA: *Oh my God. Oh my God. I'm so sorry.*

JAMIE: (*worried*) Oh no … oh God, it's half the book.

*She runs trying to catch some of them – but
a huge heap have headed into the water . . .*

JAMIE: (*calling out*) Just leave them, please, they're not important. They're not worth it. Stop, stop!

Jamie starts to head after her. She gets to the water's edge and hesitates for a moment, then whips off her dress to reveal just pants and a bra. Time slows down. Jamie watches. It's an unexpectedly lovely body under her funny old clothes.

It's all just rubbish – please, just leave it.

But she dives in.

Oh God, she's in …

He heads towards the water pulling his jumper off.

… and now she'll think I'm a total spas if I don't go in too …

AURELIA: *Fuck, it's cold!*

Jamie jumps in clumsily…

JAMIE: Fuck, it's freezing. Fuck!

They swim around after the floating papers…

AURELIA: *This stuff better be good.*

JAMIE: It's not worth it, you know, it isn't bloody Shakespeare.

AURELIA: *I don't want to drown saving some shit my grandmother could have written.*

JAMIE: Just stop! Stop!

AURELIA: *What kind of an idiot doesn't do copies?*

JAMIE: I really must do copies. You know, there better not be eels in here –
I can't stand eels…

AURELIA: *Try not to disturb the eels.*

JAMIE: Oh God – what the hell is that?

As he thinks he feels an eel.

58 INT. FARMHOUSE IN FRANCE – LIVING ROOM. DAY.

Cut to a few minutes later. Jamie comes in from the kitchen with a cup of coffee.
Aurelia is in a chair near his table with a rug over her shoulders.

JAMIE: Thank you. Thank you so much. I know,
I'll name one of the characters after you.

AURELIA: *Maybe you could name one of the characters after me. Or give me*
50 per cent of the profits.

JAMIE: Or I could give you five per cent of the profits.

AURELIA: *What kind of book is it? Kind. Kind…*

She points to the pages and mimes tears, laughter, then a heart.

JAMIE: Ah, yes.

He gets what she's saying – mimes a stabbing knife – murder.

AURELIA: *Ah – thriller… crime…*

JAMIE: Yes. Si. Crime. Murder.

AURELIA: *Frightening?*

She mimes a scared face.

JAMIE: Scary? Yes, sometimes scary – sometimes not … Mainly scary how bad
the writing is.

A slightly awkward pause. She starts to get up.

AURELIA: *I'd better get back to work. And then later you'll drive me home?*

She mimes driving… He nods 'yes'. They look at each other.

JAMIE: It's my favourite time of day, driving you.

AURELIA: *It's the saddest part of my day, leaving you.*

59 INT./EXT. JAMIE'S CAR AND FRENCH SCENERY. DAY.

They drive along. She looks at him, he looks at her – her hair still wet.
She catches him looking at her. They both look away.

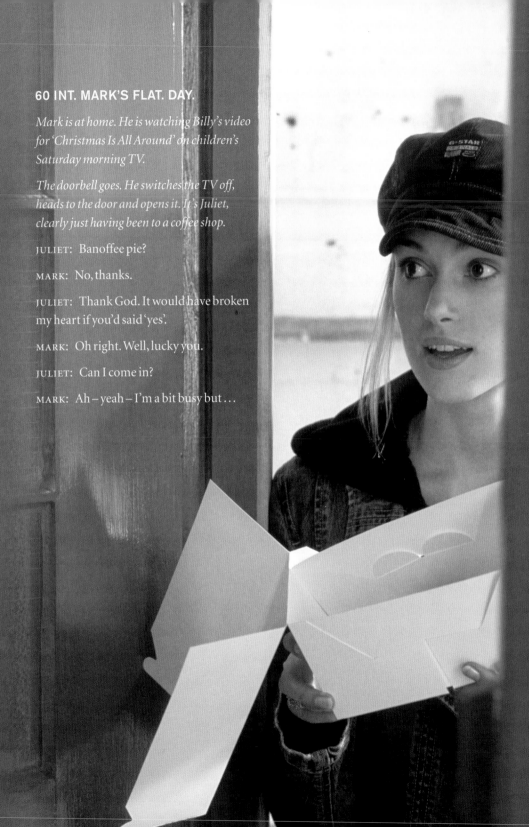

60 INT. MARK'S FLAT. DAY.

Mark is at home. He is watching Billy's video for 'Christmas Is All Around' on children's Saturday morning TV.

The doorbell goes. He switches the TV off, heads to the door and opens it. It's Juliet, clearly just having been to a coffee shop.

JULIET: Banoffee pie?

MARK: No, thanks.

JULIET: Thank God. It would have broken my heart if you'd said 'yes'.

MARK: Oh right. Well, lucky you.

JULIET: Can I come in?

MARK: Ah – yeah – I'm a bit busy but . . .

Juliet comes in anyway.

JULIET: I was just passing and thought we might check that video thing out. I thought I might be able to swap it for some pie, or maybe … (*Producing them from her pocket*) Munchies?

MARK: Actually I was being serious – I don't know where it is. I'll have a poke around tonight, and then …

JULIET: Mark – can I say something …

MARK: (*not very comfortable*) Yes …

JULIET: I know you're Peter's best friend. And I know you've never particularly warmed to me. (*He demurs*) Don't argue. We've never got … friendly. But I just wanted to say – I hope it can change. I'm nice – I really am. Apart from my terrible taste in pie. It would be good if we could be friends.

MARK: (*a bit coldly*) Absolutely. Absolutely.

JULIET: Great …

She's a bit hurt at how little he has given back – but it just sums up how little he likes her. So she heads on again …

MARK: Doesn't mean we'll be able to find the video though. I had a real search when you first called and couldn't find any trace of it, so …

JULIET: There's one here that says 'Peter and Juliet's Wedding' – do you think we might be on the right track?

MARK: Ah – yes – well – wow – that could be it.

JULIET: Do you mind if I just …

She moves towards the telly and puts the tape into the machine.

MARK: I've probably taped over it … almost everything has episodes of *West Wing* on it now …

She sits – he stands as the video starts to play. It begins with a shot of her coming down the aisle.

JULIET: Oh bingo – that's lovely. Well done you!

And a shot of her during the priestly stuff …

That's gorgeous. Thank you so much, Mark, this is exactly what I was hoping for … I look quite pretty.

He stands silently in the background. One close-up after another of Juliet. She looks around at Mark.

You've stayed rather close, haven't you …

She turns back and Mark puts his face into his hands. He's looking at her.

The camera moves to Juliet's divine laughing, blushing face … all the time. There's no one else in this video – and now everything is becoming clear.

Then Juliet during the first dance – just her face – Peter's nose just coming into frame momentarily once in a while.

And then the end of the day, Juliet dressed in going-away clothes, walking, waving goodbye.

JULIET: They're all of me.

MARK: Yeah. Yeah. Yes . . .

The tape comes to an end – turns into a flicker.

Pause. They are both frozen.

JULIET: But you never talk to me – you always talk to Peter. You don't like me.

Pause. Nothing impatient here – he just can't go there.

MARK: Hope it's useful. Don't show it around too much. It needs a bit of editing. Look, I've got to get to a . . . lunch. Early lunch. You can just show yourself out, can't you. (*He heads towards the door – then turns*) It's a self-preservation thing, you see.

61 EXT. MARK'S FLAT / LONDON STREET. DAY.

Cut to outside the house. Mark hesitates and turns to go back a couple of times but finally walks away – sad music plays. He heads through the Coin Street shops to the river's edge.

62 INT. 10 DOWNING STREET – PM'S OFFICE. DAY.

There is a knock on the door – it's Annie.

PM: Annie, my darling, my dream, my boat. I need you to do a favour for me.

ANNIE: Of course. Anything for the hero of the hour.

PM: Don't ask me why – and for heaven's sake don't read stuff into this – it's just a weird . . . personality thing. You know Natalie, who works here?

ANNIE: The chubby girl?

PM: Would we call her chubby?

ANNIE: I think there's a pretty sizeable arse there, yes, sir. Huge thighs.

PM: Well, whatever. I'm sure she's a lovely girl – but I wonder if you could redistribute her . . .

ANNIE: It's done.

She leaves. He takes in what he's done.

63 INT. DANIEL'S HOUSE – OFFICE. NIGHT.

Daniel is in his office, very late. We've caught him at a bad moment – he is looking sadly at a picture of his Joanna. The door opens – he snaps out of it, as best he can – good enough to fool Sam, who enters in his pyjamas.

DANIEL: Hey Sam-o. Can't sleep?

SAM: I got some terrible news today.

DANIEL: Let's have it.

SAM: Joanna's going back to America.

DANIEL: Your girl is American?

SAM: Yes – she's American and she's not my girl and she's going back to America and that's the end of my life as I know it.

DANIEL: That is bad news. We need Kate and we need Leo and we need them now. Come on.

64 INT. DANIEL'S HOUSE – LIVING ROOM. NIGHT.

They are watching Titanic *where Leo has taken Kate to the ship's bow to watch the sunset. He asks her, 'Do you trust me?' 'I trust you'. They stand up on the railings, their arms outstretched.*

Cut to the boys with arms outspread as well. Daniel stands behind Sam.

DANIEL: Do you trust me?

SAM: I trust you.

DANIEL: Fool!

Daniel grabs Sam and tickles him. They fall back on to the sofa laughing. Cut to a few moments later. They sit in silence.

DANIEL: Though you know, Sammy, I'm sure she's unique and extraordinary – but general wisdom is that, in the end, there isn't just one person for each of us.

SAM: There was for Kate and Leo. There was for you. There is for me. She's the one.

He lifts his finger in a distinctive 'one' movement.

DANIEL: Fair enough … And her name's Joanna?

SAM: Yeah, I know. Same as Mum.

Daniel takes this in.

65 INT. 10 DOWNING STREET – PM'S OFFICE. NIGHT.

The PM is working. A knock on the door – he almost flinches.

PM: Yes.

The door opens slowly. It is a woman with tea – not Natalie.

NEW WOMAN: Prime Minister.

PM: Thank you.

He looks at her, thinking. A possibility is gone. Sad music plays.

66 EXT. FARMHOUSE IN FRANCE. DAY.

Cut to Jamie putting his cases and lots of Frenchy presents – wine and cheese and strings of garlic, etc. in the car. Aurelia comes out of the house with more of his bags.

JAMIE: Apologia. Grande familio. Grande tradizione di Christmas presents stupidos.

67 EXT. MARSEILLES STREET. DAY.

Cut to Jamie dropping Aurelia off at the edge of the town. A cold, urban environment. He gets out with her and puts forward his hand to shake it. She takes it and shakes it. Then…

JAMIE: Well – goodbye.

AURELIA: *Thank you. I will miss you and your very slow typing…and your very bad driving…*

He smiles at her – none the wiser. So she simply leans in and kisses him gently on the mouth and walks away. He stops and thinks and then sets off again, a little dazed and confused.

He gets into his car and pulls out without looking, colliding with the car behind him.

68 EXT. LONDON STREET. DAY.

*Cut to the video of Billy's pop song – it strongly resembles
Robert Palmer's 'Addicted To Love' – but the seven sulky girls
are all dressed in tiny red Santa dresses. We see Sam's face
peering. The camera stays with Sam. He is watching the
video in the window of a record store.*

A thought goes through Sam's mind.

69 INT. DANIEL'S HOUSE – OFFICE. DAY.

Daniel is working. Sam bursts in.

SAM: Daniel! I have a plan.

DANIEL: Thank the Lord. Tell me.

SAM: Girls love musicians, don't they? Even the really weird ones get girlfriends.

DANIEL: That's right. Meatloaf definitely got laid at least once. For God's sake, Ringo Starr married a Bond girl.

SAM: Whatever, there's this big concert at the end of term – and Joanna's in it – and I thought maybe if I was in the band and played absolutely superbly, there's a chance that she might actually fall in love with me. What do you think?

DANIEL: I think it's brilliant. I think it's stellar. Apart from the one obvious, tiny little, baby little hiccough …

SAM: That I don't play a musical instrument.

DANIEL: Yes, sir.

SAM: A tiny insignificant detail.

70 INT. DANIEL'S HOUSE – CORRIDOR. NIGHT.

Loud noise of drumming. Daniel, very late at night, walks past Sam's room – from inside which comes the sound of totally obsessive, repetitive drumming. The drumming continues – and forms the basis of the music over a short montage that sees us getting closer and closer to Christmas.

71 INT. FAIRTRADE OFFICE. NIGHT.

Sarah putting up a very modern little tree-type thing on her office desk.

72 INT. GALLERY. NIGHT.

Cut inside. Music is playing and Harry's office party is in full swing.

We see Karl getting a drink and Sarah standing a bit nervously on her own, beside a huge graphic naked photo. She is looking quite lovely. Harry talks to Karen.

KAREN: I suppose I'd better do the duty round . . .

HARRY: You're a saint.

As soon as she's gone, Mia is there, tapping Harry on the shoulder. She is looking absolutely devastating, as girls can do at Christmas, with a tight red dress and a tiny pair of devil's horns.

MIA: Any chance of a dance with the boss?

HARRY: Yes, sure, sure . . . As long as your boyfriend doesn't mind.

Cut to Mark dancing with a hectic short girl.

MIA: NOT my boyfriend.

Cut to Karen elsewhere, just talking sweetly to a very dull couple. She spots Harry and Mia starting to dance.

HARRY: You're looking very . . . pretty tonight.

Little pause.

MIA: It's for you.

HARRY: Sorry?

MIA: (*leaning in close to whisper in Harry's ear*) It's all for you . . . sir.

73 INT. 10 DOWNING STREET. NIGHT.

The end of a long day – the PM is looking tired as he wanders through 10 Downing Street. A single man in a big house. He heads upstairs, and finally settles down in front of the TV, parked near a couch in the corner of a too big room.

Papers in front of him, he turns the telly on – it's Billy Mack on Parkinson.

74 INT. PARKINSON STUDIO. NIGHT.

PARKY: Well, this must be a very exciting moment for you – fighting for the Christmas Number One. How is it looking so far?

BILLY: Very bad indeed. Blue are outselling me five to one. But I'm hoping for a late surge. And if I reach Number One, I promise to sing the song stark naked on TV on Christmas Eve.

PARKY: Do you mean that?

BILLY: Of course I mean it, Michael. Want a preview, you old flirt?

He gets up and heads over to Parky, unbuttoning his trousers. Parky laughs.

PARKY: That'll never make Number One.

The audience laughs and the PM laughs too...

75 INT. GALLERY. NIGHT.

The party again. Harry and Mia are flirting and laughing together as Sarah and Karen watch on.

SARAH: I suppose it's his job to dance with everyone, isn't it?

KAREN: Some more than others.

Suddenly Karl is there.

KARL: Just one dance? Before we run out of chances.

SARAH: Who – me?

KARL: Unless you...

SARAH: No, no – good – yes – thanks.

A perky tune plays... but the second they start to dance... a romantic tune begins. They have to get closer and they seem to fit pretty well together. A moment of happiness.

76 INT. CAR. NIGHT.

Cut to Karl and Sarah in a car together – the music plays on... Sarah is still in a state of shock.

77 INT. SARAH'S FLAT – HALLWAY. NIGHT.

Later in Sarah's hallway…

KARL: Well, I better go.

SARAH: Okay.

KARL: Good-night.

SARAH: Good-night.

He kisses her – first on the cheek – and then on the lips. Pause. He's very straight-faced.

KARL: Actually, I don't have to go.

SARAH: Right. Good. That's good.

It's not that she's smug about this – it's the best moment of her life. She just mustn't leap up and scream. She tries to play it cool.

SARAH: Would you just excuse me one second?

KARL: Sure.

She walks round the corner and silently yet hysterically leaps up and down with utter delight – and then calmly walks back again.

78 INT. SARAH'S FLAT – HALLWAY. NIGHT.

SARAH: Okay, that's done. Why don't you come upstairs in about ten seconds...

KARL: Ten seconds...

79 INT. SARAH'S FLAT – BEDROOM. NIGHT.

She is tidying frantically – then Karl enters. He carefully takes off his overcoat. There's a pause and then they rush together and start kissing. Off comes his jacket and then his shirt. He awkwardly pulls her dress over her head.

Not a graphic sex scene, but what happens next is that he lies down, now only in his underwear and she sits up on him. He looks up as she continues to undress.

KARL: You're beautiful.

Soft music plays. She looks at him as he strokes her face and they kiss again. She removes her bra...

And then the phone starts to ring. They both look in its direction – Sarah hesitates, and then...

SARAH: I'd better answer that.

She leans across him to answer the phone and covers herself up. The person on the other end is talking a lot.

SARAH: Hello. Hello, darling … No, I'm not busy.

Karl looks at her – surprised and slightly hurt.

No – fire away. Right … Yes … I'm not quite sure it's going to be possible to get the Pope on the phone tonight, but … Yes, yes … I'm sure that he's very good at … exorcism.

She slips sideways off Karl and they sit apart on the bed.

Well I'm sure Jon Bon Jovi is as well and I'll definitely look into it …

Karl sits patiently on the side of the bed.

Okay – I'll talk to you later. Bye bye. (*She hangs up*) Sorry about that.

KARL: No, it's fine.

SARAH: It was my brother. He's not well. He calls a lot.

KARL: I'm sorry.

SARAH: No, it's fine. I mean, it's not really fine – it is what it is. And sort of there being no parents now and us being over here, it's my job to keep an eye on him. I mean, not my 'job' – obviously, I'm glad to do it.

KARL: That's okay – I mean, life is full of interruptions and complications. So …

He leans in and kisses her, and then we have a few more moments of romance, but then the phone goes again. She watches it ring.

KARL: Will it make him better?

SARAH: No.

KARL: Then maybe … don't answer?

Pause. She looks at Karl – and reaches over and answers.

SARAH: Hey, how you doing? Right … Right.

Karl sits quietly by the bedside.

Oh, please, oh, don't – little darling – between the two of us, we'll find the answer and it won't hurt any more …

And Karl puts his head in his hands, waiting. Sarah sits on the floor by the bed.

No, I'm not busy. Of course, if you want me to come over, I will … Okay …

She glances at Karl. Sad music plays. Only the bed between them – but they're worlds apart.

80 INT. KAREN'S HOUSE – BEDROOM. NIGHT.

The sad music continues to play over Harry and Karen in their bedroom.

KAREN: That was a good night – though I felt fat.

HARRY: Oh don't be ridiculous.

KAREN: It's true.

She slips off her dress shyly. She is a little bigger now.

Nowadays the only clothes I can get into were once owned by Pavarotti.

Cut back to Harry, watching her.

HARRY: I always think Pavarotti dresses very well.

KAREN: Mia's very pretty.

HARRY: Is she?

KAREN: You know she is, darling. Be careful there.

81 INT. MIA'S BEDROOM. NIGHT.

Mia, slipping off her dress in her seductive bedroom. Red underwear. Startling figure.

82 INT. HOSPITAL. NIGHT.

Cut to Sarah and her brother Michael in a high-security hospital ward. Very bare. A lonely room.

He is a terrible version of the young man we saw in the photo on her desk. Ghostly, pale, with dirty hair – a different weight.

They are sitting opposite each other. He just looks at her.

SARAH: Have you been watching stuff on TV?

MICHAEL: No ... Every night.

SARAH: Oh good.

MICHAEL: Every day ... The nurses are trying to kill me.

SARAH: Nobody's trying to kill you, babe.

Pause. He suddenly lifts his hand to hit her. A male nurse moves to protect her. Sarah takes the raised hand and says, very gently ...

Don't do that, my darling. Don't do that.

83 INT. KAREN'S HOUSE – BEDROOM. NIGHT.

Cut to Karen, lying awake beside Harry, very sad. She knows in some way she's lost him. She looks across at him, then turns over, a tiny tear gathered in her eye.

84 INT. FAIRTRADE OFFICE. DAY.

Next day. A slightly post-party mood. Harry comes out of his office. Mia is sitting at her desk.

HARRY: Right. Back at three – Christmas shopping – never an easy or a pleasant task.

He heads out – but just before he's gone ...

MIA: Are you going to get me something?

HARRY: Ahm – I don't know – I hadn't thought.

There's a new sexual tension between them.

Where's Sarah by the way?

MIA: She couldn't make it in today. A family thing.

HARRY: There's a word for hangover I've never heard before. See you later.

MIA: Yes. Looking forward to it. A lot.

And he heads out, all perplexed by how he's feeling.

85 EXT. LONDON STREET. DAY.

Cut to Harry walking down the street – it's all hugely Christmassy now – trees and lights everywhere. He thinks – then fatally and casually takes out his mobile phone and speed dials.

HARRY: So – are you going to give *me* something?

MIA: I thought I'd made it clear last night. When it comes to me, you can have everything.

86 EXT. LONDON STREET. DAY.

Back to Harry now in a bustling square, on his mobile.

HARRY: So – ahm – what do you need – something along the stationery line – are you short of staplers?

MIA: No, I don't want something I need. I want something I want. Something pretty.

HARRY: Right. Right …

He closes his phone – disturbed by this exchange. Then spots Karen in the crowd and waves.

KAREN: Sorry I'm late – had to drop off Bernie at rehearsal.

87 INT. SELFRIDGES DEPARTMENT STORE. DAY.

KAREN: Right – you keep yourself occupied for ten minutes while I do the boring stuff for our mothers.

She heads off. He quickly looks around – and sees the jewellery section. Pauses – and heads for it. He reaches a counter and sees exactly what he wants. The person serving is busy – but then suddenly, a new voice …

RUFUS: Looking for anything in particular, sir?

He is a very particular looking man, very accurate, slightly camp, with a very particular tie.

HARRY: Yes … ahm. That necklace there … how much is it?

RUFUS: It's £270.

HARRY: *(this is a moral as well as financial decision)* All right. I'll have it.

It is a beautiful, delicate gold heart necklace.

RUFUS: Lovely. Would you like it gift-wrapped?

HARRY: Yes, all right.

RUFUS: Lovely.

He takes the necklace out – and puts it in a little box.

Just pop it in the box … there.

HARRY: Look, could we be quite quick.

RUFUS: Certainly, sir. Ready in the flashiest of flashes.

In a very trained manner he cuts two feet of the ribbon – wraps it round the box – then wraps it round again. Then ties it.

There.

HARRY: That's great.

RUFUS: Not quite finished.

Rufus opens a drawer – and takes out a see-through cellophane bag. All the while, Harry is looking round nervously.

HARRY: Look, actually, I don't need a bag – I can just put it in my pocket.

RUFUS: This isn't a bag, sir.

HARRY: Really?

RUFUS: This is so much more than a bag.

He opens the bag, opens another drawer, and takes out little dried roses. Harry continues to look worried.

HARRY: Could we be quite quick ... please.

RUFUS: Prontissimo.

Then some lavender – and sprinkles it in the bag. Then he opens another drawer – and takes out a four-inch stick of cinnamon.

HARRY: What's that?

RUFUS: It's a cinnamon stick, sir.

HARRY: Actually, I really can't wait.

RUFUS: You won't regret it, sir.

HARRY: Want a bet?

Looking round more frantically ...

RUFUS: 'Tis but the work of a moment.

He twists the top of the bag and ties the cinnamon stick on it.

There. Almost finished.

HARRY: Almost finished? What else can there be – are you going to dip it in yoghurt and cover it with chocolate buttons?

RUFUS: No, sir. We're going to pop it in this Christmas box.

HARRY: But I don't WANT a Christmas box.

RUFUS: But you said you wanted it gift-wrapped, sir.

HARRY: I did – but …

RUFUS: This is the final flourish …

HARRY: Can I just pay?

He is looking desperately round. Rufus is putting on a protective glove …

RUFUS: All I need now is a sprig of holly …

HARRY: NO! No! ! No bloody holly!

RUFUS: But sir …

HARRY: Leave it – leave it, just leave it.

Because sure enough, Karen is right there. Harry bounces away from the counter.

KAREN: Loitering round the jewellery section, I see.

HARRY: No – I was just looking.

Rufus is bitterly disappointed.

KAREN: Don't worry – my expectations are not that high after thirteen years, Mr Oh-But-You-Always-Love-Scarves …

They walk out of the store.

88 INT./EXT. TONY'S FLAT. DAY.

We see Colin outside a slightly tacky flat. It's raining. He rings a doorbell. Tony opens the door to a soaking, backpack-carrying Colin. It's a pretty small, unimpressive, very single man's flat.

COLIN: Hey!

TONY: What are you doing here?

COLIN: Had to rent out my flat to pay for the ticket.

TONY: You're not actually going ahead with this genuinely stupid plan?

COLIN: Bloody am. Think this backpack is full of clothes? Like hell it is – it's chock-a-block full of condoms.

89 INT. FILM STUDIO. DAY.

John and Judy on the set, this time a gilded bathroom. She is miming a blow-job.

TONY: Excellent. Excellent. Perfect. Keep that going.

JOHN: Look, ahm…sorry for being a bit forward, but you don't fancy going for a Christmas drink, you know, nothing implied – we could just maybe go and see something Christmassy or something…obviously you don't have to if you don't want to…I was just…I'm rambling now.

JUDY: No, that'd be lovely.

JOHN: Oh great.

90 INT. FILM STUDIO. NIGHT.

And cut on to the next position. She sits on, or at least near, his face.

JOHN: That is really great. Normally I'm really shy about this sort of thing – takes me ages to get the courage up – so thank you.

91 INT. DANIEL'S HOUSE – CORRIDOR. NIGHT.

Daniel passes the door of Sam's room, still drumming. He winces.

92 INT. KAREN'S HOUSE. NIGHT.

Karen is whipping off Harry's coat…

KAREN: Explain to me again why you're so late?

HARRY: Oh for heaven's sake, woman – can't a man have any secrets?

KAREN: Well, hurry up, we've been waiting for hours. It's the first-ever preview.

She goes to hang up his coat. In the pocket she feels something – and takes it out – it is a small flat box. She opens it – it has a delicate gold necklace in it. She smiles and puts it back, then heads into the living room – where a now total body-suit lobster and very hip angel await. Harry, the audience, is sat and ready.

'It was a starry night in ancient Jerusalem, and the baby Jesus was in his manger.'

93 INT. LANGUAGE SCHOOL. NIGHT.

Cut to a huge, neon-lit room. It's full of people at formica desks listening to tapes, with big earphones. We pan across people learning English, from every corner of the world.

LANGUAGE STUDENT 1: Sherlock Holmes is not a real detective.

LANGUAGE STUDENT 2: *(in Russian) Is this the way to the train station?*

LANGUAGE STUDENT 3: I would like half a pound of cherries.

LANGUAGE STUDENT 4: I would like a one-day travel card.

And one of the students is Jamie, practising out loud – but it's not English he's learning. It's Portuguese.

JAMIE: *(in Portuguese) I've got a terrible stomach ache. It must have been the prawns.*

LANGUAGE STUDENT 5: Milton Keynes has many roundabouts.

94 INT/EXT. UNDERGROUND STATION. DAY.

An underground station escalator. A group of people are coming past the camera – one of them is Jamie. He gets closer and we see he is wearing earphones, and apparently talking to himself – trying to act convincingly, even if not sounding very, Portuguese . . .

JAMIE: *My goodness, this is a very big fish! It tastes delicious.*

He's also carrying some Christmas present bags – this is clearly someone who takes Christmas seriously.

95 INT. KAREN'S HOUSE – LIVING ROOM. NIGHT.

Another tree. It's Karen late at night. She picks up a square package, wrapped in white with gold stars. She smiles. It twinkles like the Holy Grail.

There's a card. She opens it. Her husband's handwriting.

'Sorry I'm such a grumpy bugger XX Bad Harry.'

The package is exactly the size of the necklace case – she's very delighted.

96 INT. HEATHROW AIRPORT. DAY.

Cut to Heathrow Airport. Tony and Colin are just coming up the escalator.

TONY: You'll come back a broken man.

COLIN: Yeah, back broken – from too much sex.

TONY: You are on the road to disaster.

COLIN: No, I am on Shag Highway, heading west.

As Colin heads towards customs he shouts these final words …

Farewell, failure! America – watch out! Here comes Colin Frissell! And he's got a big knob!

97 EXT. MILWAUKEE AIRPORT / WISCONSIN. NIGHT.

We see a view of the airport from the outside. Total snow.

98 EXT/INT. MILWAUKEE AIRPORT / WISCONSIN – CAB. NIGHT.

Colin gets into a cab.

COLIN: Take me to a bar.

TAXI DRIVER: What kind of bar?

COLIN: Just any bar – just your average American bar.

99 INT. BAR IN WISCONSIN. NIGHT.

He heads in – there's not much going on – a typical American bar – just a juke-box and a game of pool. He goes to the bar.

BARMAN: Can I help you?

COLIN: Yes – I'd like a Budweiser please. King of beers.

BARMAN: One Bud coming up.

A girl sits at the bar next to him.

STACEY: Oh my God, are you from England?

He turns and looks at her – she's exquisite. Just imagine the most gorgeous American girl you've ever seen …

COLIN: Yes.

STACEY: That is so cute. Hi – I'm Stacey. (*She calls out*) Jeannie!

Her best friend turns round from the juke-box. She's also completely stunning.

JEANNIE: Yeah?

STACEY: This is ...

COLIN: Colin ... Frissell.

JEANNIE: Cute name. Jeannie.

STACEY: He's from England.

COLIN: Yup. Basildon.

They're impressed.

JEANNIE: Wait till Carol Anne gets here – she's crazy about English guys.

The door opens. Enter a third beauty. Every girl in America is more beautiful than every single girl in Britain.

CAROL ANNE: Hey girls.

JEANNIE: Carol Anne – come meet Colin. He's from England.

CAROL ANNE: Well, step aside ladies – this one's on me. Hey, gorgeous.

Colin has an insanely huge grin on his face.

100 INT. BAR IN WISCONSIN. NIGHT.

Later that night, the four of them are still drinking and laughing together.

STACEY: That is so funny! What do you call that?

She points at a bottle.

COLIN: Bottle.

ALL THREE GIRLS: (*in mock English accents*) Bottle!

CAROL ANNE: What about this?

She points to a straw.

COLIN: Straw.

ALL THREE GIRLS: Straw!

JEANNIE: What about this?

She taps the table.

COLIN: Table.

All three girls draw breath to repeat it…

JEANNIE: Table – it's the same.

CAROL ANNE: Where are you staying?

COLIN: Ahm, I don't actually know – guess I'll just 'check into a motel' like they do in the movies…

STACEY: Oh my God, oh my God, that is so cute.

JEANNIE: Listen, this may be a bit pushy because we've just met you – but why don't you come back and sleep at our place?

COLIN: Ahm…Well, I mean, you know – if it's not too much of an inconvenience…

CAROL ANNE: Hell, no. But there's one problem.

COLIN: What?

JEANNIE: Well, we're not the richest of girls, so we just have a little bed, and no couch – so you'd have to share with all three of us…

CAROL ANNE: And on this cold, cold night, it's going to be crowded and sweaty, and stuff.

STACEY: And we can't even afford pyjamas.

JEANNIE: Which means…we would be naked.

Pause as girls look embarrassed.

COLIN: No, no, I think it'd be fine.

CAROL ANNE: And you know what's going to make it even more crowded – Harriet. You haven't met Harriet.

COLIN: There's a fourth one?

STACEY: Yeah – don't worry, you're totally going to like her – because she is the 'sexy one' (*does inverted commas with her fingers*).

COLIN: Really? Wow. Praise the Lord.

JEANNIE: And he's a Christian.

101 EXT. HOUSE IN WISCONSIN. NIGHT.

Music swells up as we cut to a little hokey American house covered in gaudy Christmas lights and decorations. A girl walks up to the front door – she has gorgeous legs below her micro-skirt. Colin is silhouetted against the top window being undressed by the three girls before they fall on to the bed out of sight.

102 INT. KAREN'S HOUSE – LIVING ROOM. NIGHT.

Christmas is really in swing now – it's present-opening time at Karen's.

KAREN: One present only each tonight. Who's got one for Dad?

BERNIE: I have.

HARRY: No, let Mummy go first.

KAREN: No, no, no, I want to choose mine. I think I want this one.

It's Harry's present.

HARRY: Ah – now – I have, of course, bought the traditional scarf as well – but this is my other … slightly special, personal one.

KAREN: Thank you – that's a real first.

She opens it, smiling, full of excitement and love. It is … a CD of Joni Mitchell.

KAREN: That's a surprise ... It's a CD – Joni Mitchell. Wow.

HARRY: To continue your emotional education.

KAREN: Yes. Goodness. That's great.

HARRY: My brilliant wife.

KAREN: Ha! Yes. Actually, do you mind if I just absent myself for a second. All that ice-cream. Darling – could you just make sure the kids are ready to go. I'll be back in a minute.

She moves slowly out of the room with a slightly glazed smile. A slightly mysterious musical sound starts ...

103 INT. MIA'S BEDROOM. NIGHT.

Mia in her underwear gets up from her unmade bed and sits in front of a mirror, putting on the gold heart necklace.

104 INT. KAREN'S HOUSE – BEDROOM. NIGHT.

Cut to Karen in her bedroom. She's just standing there – rigid – listening to Joni, playing 'Both Sides Now' loud on the CD player.

Tears fall from her eyes.

She dries her tears and tries to smile – and as the song continues, heads back to rejoin family life.

105 INT. KAREN'S HOUSE – HALLWAY/LIVING ROOM. NIGHT.

Karen gathers herself before she walks through into the living room, where she gets straight back to family business, with smiles and kisses ... and a breaking heart.

106 INT. DANIEL'S HOUSE – LIVING ROOM. NIGHT.

Sam and Daniel are lying head to head on the sofa.

DANIEL: Has she noticed you yet?

SAM: No – but you know the thing about romances – people only get together right at the very end ...

DANIEL: Of course.

SAM: By the way – I feel bad I never ask you how your love life's going.

DANIEL: Ha! No. As you know, that was a done deal long ago. Unless of course, Claudia Schiffer calls … in which case I want you out of this house straight away, you wee motherless mongrel. We'll want to have sex in every room – including yours.

107 EXT. LONDON SKYLINE. NIGHT.

The next day – Christmas Eve – the camera moves across London. The Radio 1 Chartshow is broadcasting to the nation …

SUNDAY DJ: And it's a rainy Christmas Eve all over the UK – and the big question is – who is Number One on the Radio 1 Chartshow tonight – is it Blue, or the unexpected Christmas sensation from Billy Mack? Well, you might have guessed it although you may not believe it. It's … Billy Mack!

108 INT. RECORD COMPANY BOARDROOM. NIGHT.

The room is totally packed with record people, all going berserk. 'Yes, yes, yes!' Joe stands at the back.

JOE: You are the champion!

Billy stands on a table in the middle of the room and talks on the phone.

BILLY: Hello.

SUNDAY DJ: Hello Billy. We're live across the nation and you're Number One. How will you be celebrating?

BILLY: I don't know – either I could behave like a real rock and roll loser and get drunk with my fat manager – or when I hang up, I'll be flooded by invitations to a large number of glamorous parties.

SUNDAY DJ: Let's hope it's the latter. And here it is – Number One – from Billy Mack . . . It's 'Christmas Is All Around'.

BILLY: Oh Jesus – not that crap again!

He hangs up. Gina, a young frisky record executive, steps forward, holding her mobile.

GINA: Bill – it's for you, babe.

He takes the phone.

BILLY: Hello? Elton. Of course. Of course. Of course. Send an embarrassingly big car and I'll be there.

He hangs up.

It's going to be a very good Christmas.

Joe is a bit lost now in the crowd of Billy's new friends.

109 EXT. JUDY'S FLAT. NIGHT.

Cut to Judy and John outside her front door, fully clothed, at the end of their first date. Nervous.

JUDY: I better be getting inside, actually. My Mum and . . .

JOHN: Yes, it's getting a bit cold. Well, goodnight.

JUDY: Night.

Pause. Pause. Pause. John looks like he's going to kiss her and then appears to lose his nerve. So she leans forward and gives him an awkward but tender parting kiss. He is dazzled.

All I want for Christmas is you.

JOHN: Right - thank you. Good. Bye . . . goodnight.

She slips back into the house and closes the door – he turns from the door – then leaps down the steps, ecstatic.

110 EXT. JAMIE'S PARENTS' HOUSE. NIGHT.

Jamie walks to the door, carrying bags full of presents – he rings the doorbell.

111 INT. JAMIE'S PARENTS' HOUSE. NIGHT.

The door opens.

JAMIE'S SISTER: Look, everyone – it's Uncle Jamie.

Instantly a vast number of family members of all ages greet him. Huge excitement.

JAMIE: Yes – splendid – lovely to see you all. And . . . I'm off actually.

JAMIE'S MUM: But, Jamie, darling . . .

JAMIE: Sorry – a man's gotta do what a man's gotta do.

He hands his sister the bags full of presents and leaves.

CHILD 1: I hate Uncle Jamie.

CHILD 2: I hate Uncle Jamie.

CHILD 3: I HATE Uncle Jamie!

112 EXT. STREET. NIGHT.

Very busy Christmas street. Jamie is hailing a cab.

JAMIE: Gatwick Airport, please. Fast as you can.

113 INT. FAIRTRADE OFFICE. NIGHT.

Karl gets up to leave and walks towards Sarah's desk. They are the only two left in the office this late.

KARL: Good-night, Sarah.

SARAH: Good-night, Karl.

KARL: I...

*He looks like he's going to say
something about what happened,
but he just can't find the words.*

...Merry Christmas.

*Sarah smiles gently at him.
All the possibility has gone.*

SARAH: Merry Christmas.

*He leaves. Tears well up in her
eyes as, for the first time, she is
the one who dials her mobile.
She tries to sound cheerful,
in spite of her broken heart.*

Hi babe – how you doing?
Is it all party, party, party
down there?

114 INT. 10 DOWNING STREET – DRAWING ROOM. NIGHT.

The PM is pottering around a big room, still leafing through his big work pile in his brief case. He comes across a bunch of Christmas cards . . . with a note from his secretary on a post-it note: 'Read these – a random sample.'

He considers it, then puts them aside and works on.

115 INT. DANIEL'S HOUSE – CORRIDOR. NIGHT

Cut to Daniel upstairs outside Sam's room.

DANIEL: Sam, time for dinner.

SAM: I'm not hungry.

DANIEL: Sam, I've done chicken kebabs.

SAM: Look at the sign on the door.

It says 'I said – I'm not hungry.'

DANIEL: Right.

116 INT. HOSPITAL. NIGHT.

Sarah and her brother – they sit in the hospital unwrapping presents. Michael leans forward to hug her. She hugs him back. It's love too.

117 INT./EXT. JULIET AND PETER'S HOUSE. NIGHT.

Inside Peter and Juliet are sitting watching telly . . . the doorbell rings. Juliet gets up.

JULIET: I'll get it.

She leaves the living room, goes down the stairs and opens the front door. It's Mark.

JULIET: Oh, hi.

PETER (V/O): Who is it?

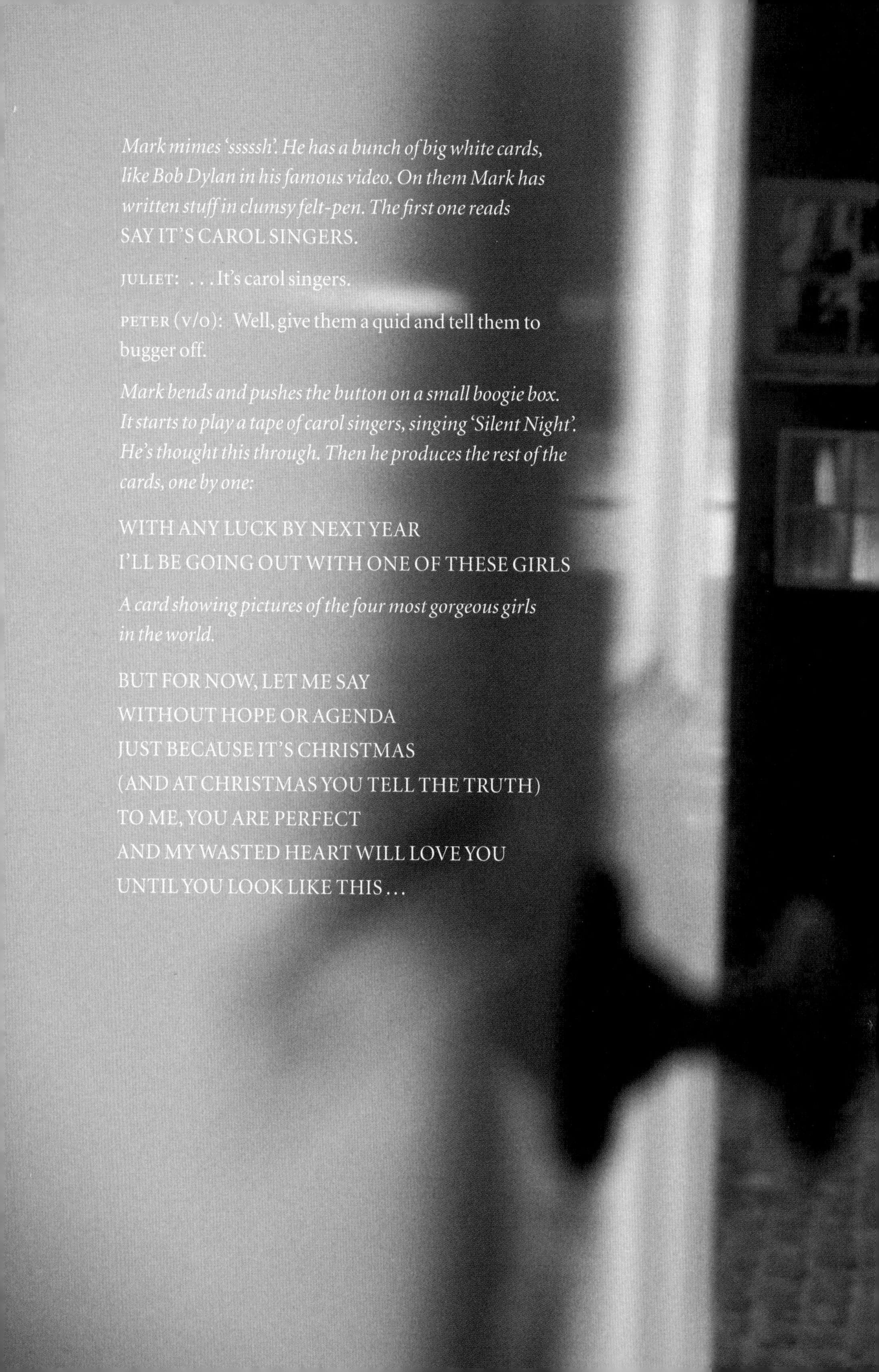

Mark mimes 'sssssh'. He has a bunch of big white cards,
like Bob Dylan in his famous video. On them Mark has
written stuff in clumsy felt-pen. The first one reads
SAY IT'S CAROL SINGERS.

JULIET: . . . It's carol singers.

PETER (V/O): Well, give them a quid and tell them to
bugger off.

Mark bends and pushes the button on a small boogie box.
It starts to play a tape of carol singers, singing 'Silent Night'.
He's thought this through. Then he produces the rest of the
cards, one by one:

WITH ANY LUCK BY NEXT YEAR
I'LL BE GOING OUT WITH ONE OF THESE GIRLS

A card showing pictures of the four most gorgeous girls
in the world.

BUT FOR NOW, LET ME SAY
WITHOUT HOPE OR AGENDA
JUST BECAUSE IT'S CHRISTMAS
(AND AT CHRISTMAS YOU TELL THE TRUTH)
TO ME, YOU ARE PERFECT
AND MY WASTED HEART WILL LOVE YOU
UNTIL YOU LOOK LIKE THIS . . .

He holds up a picture of a mummified corpse.

MERRY CHRISTMAS

She mouths back 'Merry Christmas'.

He gives her a little thumbs-up – and turns away, taking the boogie box.

Suddenly a tap on his shoulder. He turns. Juliet has run after him, and gently kisses him on the lips. He smiles and walks away.

MARK: Enough. Enough now.

118 INT. JOE'S FLAT. NIGHT.

And there's Joe in his room. He's got a bottle of champagne open and he's drinking on his own, watching Billy's video on TV, like the fan he has always been and still is. The doorbell goes.

119 INT. JOE'S FLAT. NIGHT.

JOE: What the hell are you doing here? You're supposed to be at Elton John's.

BILLY: I was there for a minute or two – and then I had an epiphany.

JOE: Really. Come on – come up.

Cut into Joe's living room.

So what was this epiphany?

BILLY: It was about Christmas.

JOE: You realized that it was all around.

BILLY: No, I realized that Christmas is a time to be with the people you love.

JOE: Right.

BILLY: And I realized that – as dire chance and fateful cock-up would have it – here I am, mid-fifties and without knowing it, I've gone and spent most of my adult life with a chubby employee. And much as it grieves me to say it, it might be that the people I love is, in fact, you.

JOE: Well, this is a surprise.

BILLY: Yeah.

JOE: Ten minutes at Elton John's and you're as gay as a maypole.

BILLY: No – I'm serious here. I left Elton's place where there were a hefty number of half-naked chicks with their mouths open in order to hang out with you. At Christmas.

Pause.

JOE: Well, Bill…

BILLY: It's a terrible, terrible mistake, Chubs – but you turn out to be the fucking love of my life. And, to be honest, despite all my complaining – we have had a wonderful life.

Joe is actually deeply moved.

JOE: Well, thank you … It's been an honour. I feel very proud.

He sticks out his hand for a sentimental handshake.

BILLY: Oh, don't be a moron.

And gives him a huge bear hug.

Come on, let's get pissed and watch porn.

120 INT. 10 DOWNING STREET – DRAWING ROOM. NIGHT.

Back to the PM. Still alone. He spots the Christmas cards again. He picks them up casually.

First a couple of boring ones – the third one jolts him – it is from Natalie. He reads it. It says this …

NATALIE (V/O): Dear Sir – Dear David – Merry Christmas and I hope you have a very Happy New Year – I'm very sorry about the thing that happened. It was a very odd moment and I feel like a prize idiot. Particularly because (if you can't say it at Christmas, when can you, eh?) – I'm actually yours, with LOVE. xxx Your Natalie.

He pauses. Puts it down. Rereads it. He makes up his mind. Picks up a phone, pushes one button.

PM: Jack, I need a car. Right now. Thank you.

Big music starts to play. He leaves the drawing room.

121 INT. 10 DOWNING STREET. NIGHT.

He runs down the staircase, through the empty inner lobby and out towards the front door. There's a security person there.

PM: Don't wait up.

122 EXT. 10 DOWNING STREET. NIGHT.

He gets into the car outside 10 Downing Street – a dark, blowy night.

PM: I'd like to go to Wandsworth. The dodgy end.

123 EXT. PM'S CAR – ALBERT BRIDGE. NIGHT.

*We see the PM's car, accompanied by a police car with blue
light flashing, heading south across the river.*

**124 INT./EXT. PM'S CAR – WANDSWORTH
STREET. NIGHT.**

*The PM and his cars arrive in Wandsworth and turn
into a long street of near identical houses.*

DRIVER: Harris Street. What number, sir?

PM: Oh, God – I've got absolutely no idea
and it's the longest street in the world.

125 EXT. HARRIS STREET. NIGHT.

The PM gets out to begin the search for Natalie – he rings the doorbell of number one, Harris Street – he has with him a bodyguard, who is five yards away, discreet. An old lady opens the door.

PM: Hello. Does Natalie live here?

OLD LADY: No.

PM: Right, fine. Thank you. Sorry to disturb.

OLD LADY: Aren't you the Prime Minister?

PM: Yes – in fact I am. Merry Christmas. Part of the service now. Trying to get round everyone by New Year's Eve.

Cut to him ringing on the next door. Three very little girls answer.

PM: Hello. Does Natalie live here?

LITTLE GIRL 1: No, she doesn't.

PM: Oh dear, okay.

LITTLE GIRL 1: Are you singing carols?

PM: Ah, no, I'm not.

LITTLE GIRL 2: Please sir, please.

LITTLE GIRL 3: Please.

PM: Well, I mean, I suppose I could.

LITTLE GIRL 3: Please.

PM: Ahm … All right.

ALL THREE LITTLE GIRLS: Hooray! Hooray!

PM: 'Good King Wenceslas looked out on the Feast of Stephen …' (*He gestures towards the bodyguard, who joins in heartily*) 'When the snow lay round about, deep and crisp and even. Brightly shone the moon that night …'

The kids are dancing, loving it.

Cut – the PM knocks on another door – number 100. It opens. There is Mia. And on her neck, that necklace.

PM: Sorry to disturb – does Natalie live here?

MIA: No – she's next door.

PM: Oh brilliant.

MIA: You're not who I think you are, are you?

PM: Yes, I'm afraid I am. Sorry about all the cock-ups – not my fault – my Cabinet are absolute crap – we hope to do better next year. Merry Christmas to you.

The PM runs his hand through his hair, then, walks slowly and fatefully round to the next house. Finally he reaches it and rings the bell.

126 INT. NATALIE'S HOUSE. NIGHT.

The door opens – and a whole, explosive family is crowded into a thin corridor, all in their winter coats, obviously just seconds before all going out. It couldn't be more awkward – they're all there, nine people – and not Natalie.

PM: Hello, is Natalie in?

Natalie hasn't seen him and is coming downstairs.

NATALIE: Where the fuck is my fucking coat? Oh hello.

PM: Hello.

Big awkwardness.

NATALIE: This is my Mum and my Dad and my Uncle Tony and my Auntie Glynne…

PM: Very nice to meet you.

NATALIE: And this is… the Prime Minister…

MUM: Yes, we can see that, darling.

NATALIE: …and unfortunately we're very late.

MUM: It's the school Christmas concert, you see, David, and it's the first time all the local schools have joined together, even St Basil's, which is most…

NATALIE: Too much detail, Mum.

DAD: Anyway… ahm… how can we help, sir?

PM: Well, I just needed Natalie… on some state business.

DAD: Right, yes – of course. (*He looks at his watch*) Right, well, perhaps you should come on later, Plumpy… erm… Natalie…

PM: No – look, I don't want to make you late for the concert.

NATALIE: No, it's nothing really.

MUM: Keith'll be very disappointed.

NATALIE: No, really – it doesn't matter…

MUM: The octopus costume has taken me months. Eight is a lot of legs, David…

PM: Listen – why don't I give you a lift and then we can talk about this 'state business' business in the car?

That's not bad news for Natalie.

NATALIE: Okay.

MUM & DAD: Lovely.

127 INT./EXT. PM'S CAR – WANDSWORTH. NIGHT.

We see the police car is totally full of family.

POLICEMAN: Hold tight, everybody.

Cut into the PM's car behind – the PM, Natalie and her brother Keith sitting between them. Dressed as an octopus.

PM: How far is this place?

NATALIE: Just round the corner.

PM: Right – well, I just wanted to say – thank you for the Christmas card.

NATALIE: You're welcome … (*Then out it comes in a splurge*) Look, I'm so sorry about that day – I mean I came into the room, and he slinked towards me and there was a fire and he's the President of the United States and . . . nothing happened, I promise – and I just felt such a fool because … I think about you all the time actually, and I think that you're the man I really …

OCTOPUS KEITH: We're here!!!!

NATALIE: (*whispers so quietly the PM doesn't hear*) … love.

PM: Wow – that really was just round the corner.

The octopus climbs awkwardly over the PM, struggling to get out of the car.

Look, I think I'd better not come in – the last thing anyone wants is some sleazy politician stealing the kids' thunder.

NATALIE: No, please come. It'll be great.

PM: No, I better not. But I will be very sorry to drive away from you.

NATALIE: Just give me one second …

128 EXT. SCHOOL – CAR PARK. NIGHT.

She jumps out of the car and runs towards the school, through the car park, which is full of action.

Then cut to Judy and John, with John's brother. There's a little nephew there.

JOHN'S BROTHER: John's been very mysterious – where did you two meet?

JUDY: Ahm …

JOHN: Uhm …

Daniel and Sam are arriving – Sam carrying drumsticks – very determined looking. Daniel tries unsuccessfully to make Sam's hair look a little less fashionable.

129 EXT. MARSEILLES AIRPORT – ARRIVALS GATE. NIGHT.

A sign says Aéroport Marseilles. Jamie exits below it. He sees a taxi – but at the same moment an oldish woman walks towards it. His English politeness gets the better of him, and he lets her take the cab. Then jumps up and down in frustration at what he's done. But instantly, another cab turns up – he leaps in.

130 EXT. SCHOOL – CAR PARK. NIGHT.

Natalie comes back to the car.

NATALIE: Come on in – we can watch from backstage.

Little pause.

PM: Okay. Terry, I won't be long.

As they step out, as ever with the bodyguard, he pauses in a moment of clarity.

This has to be a very secret visit, okay?

NATALIE: Don't worry – this was my school, I know my way around. Come on.

They set off to another, not busy gate.

131 INT. SCHOOL – CORRIDOR/BACKSTAGE. NIGHT.

Back at school – Karen, the kids and Harry are late – she's having trouble moving her brood down the corridor. The PM, Natalie and the bodyguard are also going down a little corridor – in a sort of backstage area … and then the two parties bump into each other …

KAREN: David!

She hugs him. And stays hugging him a bit longer than you'd expect. Suddenly the emotion comes out. He's surprised by her intensity.

PM: How are you? Hi guys. (*Waving to his niece and nephew*) Are you all right?

KAREN: What the hell are you doing here?

PM: Well, you know, I …

KAREN: I always tell your secretary's secretary's secretary these things are going on – but it never occurred to me you'd actually turn up …

PM: Well, I thought it was about time I did. I just didn't want everyone to see, so I'm just going to hide myself somewhere and watch the show – good luck, Daisy – good luck, Bernie.

KAREN: I have to say – I've never been gladder to see my stupid big brother. Thank you.

PM: You're welcome.

KAREN: Now, we haven't been introduced.

Natalie can't go on standing there any longer. The PM plays for time.

PM: This is Gavin, my copper. And this is Natalie – who's my … er … catering manager.

NATALIE: Hi.

KAREN: Catering manager – well, watch out he keeps his hands off you – twenty years ago you would have been just his type.

They all laugh.

NATALIE: I'll be very careful. (*To the PM*) Don't try something, sir, just because it's Christmas …

A bell goes – the show's starting.

KAREN: Show time. Quickly. See you after.

PM: Yeah, probably.

KAREN: Thank you, Prime Minister.

The PM and Natalie head off and enter a sort of backstage area, full of ropes and pulleys.

132 INT. SCHOOL HALL. NIGHT.

Cut into the concert – it's the climax of a Nativity scene. The cast are singing 'Catch a Falling Star'.

There is Jesus, surrounded by Mary, Joseph and angels. Widen to take in the cast of cows, sheep, and lots and lots of sea creatures – lobsters, prawns, an octopus, a blue whale and, for no reason, Spiderman.

133 INT. SCHOOL HALL. NIGHT.

A modest teacher comes through the curtain to make an announcement.

MR TRENCH: Hillier School would now like to present their chosen Christmas number. Lead vocals by ten-year-old Joanna Anderson.

Daniel raises an eyebrow – this is her…

Backing vocals co-ordinated by her mother, the great Mrs Jean Anderson. Some of the staff have decided to help out, and for this we ask you to forgive us. Thank you.

The song begins in darkness – the tinkling of innocent Christmas bells and then in the spotlight appears the lead singer…

She is a fabulous ten-year-old girl. A slow magnificent start, Whitney meets Mariah …

And the PM and Natalie, quite close to the stage now, peer through from the wings.

The parents are all taken aback by her fantastic voice. And then it kicks into
'All I Want For Christmas Is You'. It is stunning. She is stunning.

Sam's monotonous drums suddenly make fantastic Phil Spector sense.

The head of the backing vocals is a mighty woman, clearly Joanna's mum, supported by self-conscious staff members, letting their hair down for the first time this century. Behind them a choir of kids. At one moment Daniel looks towards Sam and sends a distinctive 'she's the one' finger – Sam nods with a smile.

The PM and Natalie are watching from backstage – although when someone approaches, he puts his hand round her waist to guide her further back behind the curtain.

It is an exuberant, fabulous end to the show – some parents start to stand – Daniel and then Harry are hot on their heels – eventually everyone is standing ... John and Judy are having a particularly funky time, both dancing quite badly on the balcony. In the darkness backstage, the PM and Natalie are moving closer and closer together.

Finally Joanna reaches the last 'All I Want For Christmas Is You' – and she points and stares straight at Sam. It is the moment we've been waiting for ... But then – she moves on, 'And you ... and you ... and you ...'. Sam's smile disappears – his dreams defeated.

Hysteria just before the end – the audience explodes into applause …

Finally the stage backdrop goes up to reveal the little surprise – a full painted winter wonderland, saying 'Merry Christmas', clearly done by all the children. Fake snow starts to flutter down.

A slightly bigger surprise is that, standing there in the middle of the stage, thinking they are backstage and totally private, the PM and Natalie are kissing – instantly out come the cameras of every single parent in the school, it is a thunder and lightning of flashes … there is nothing the PM and Natalie can do.

PM: Right. So not quite as secret as we'd hoped …

NATALIE: What do we do now?

PM: Smile.

They both smile awkwardly.

Take a bow.

They both bow. The audience starts to applaud.

And a wave.

They both wave – and leave the stage.

134 INT. SCHOOL HALL. NIGHT.

Harry waits while Karen says goodbye to some other parents. She joins him. Then, casually …

KAREN: Tell me – if you were in my position – what would you do?

HARRY: What position is that?

KAREN: Imagine your husband bought a gold necklace and, come Christmas, gave it to somebody else.

HARRY: Oh Karen.

KAREN: Would you wait around to find out if it's just a necklace – or if it's sex and a necklace – or if worst of all, if it's a necklace and love? Would you stay, knowing life will always be a little bit worse? Or would you cut and run?

HARRY: Oh God. I am so in the wrong. A classic fool.

KAREN: Yes – but you've also made a fool out of me – you've made the life I lead foolish too.

At which moment, Bernie and Daisy approach full of post-concert radiance. She immediately kicks into her mother job. Harry watches her doing the thing he has almost undone.

KAREN: Darlings – you were wonderful – and my little lobster – you were so – what is that word – orange. Come on, I've got treats at home. Dad's coming.

135 INT. SCHOOL – CORRIDOR. NIGHT.

Afterwards in the school corridor the atmosphere is explosive and excited. Daniel bursts through the doors to find Sam.

DANIEL: Sammy! Fantastic show. Classic drumming, son.

SAM: Thanks. Plan didn't work though.

DANIEL: Tell her then.

SAM: Tell her what?

DANIEL: Tell her that you love her.

SAM: No way. Anyway, they fly tonight.

DANIEL: Even better. Sam, you've got nothing to lose – and you'll always regret it if you don't. I never told your mum enough – I should have told her every day, because she was perfect every day. You've seen the films, kiddo – it ain't over till it's over.

Pause.

SAM: Okay – Dad, let's do it. Let's go get the shit kicked out of us by love . . .

DANIEL: Yes!

SAM: Just give me one sec . . .

He runs off. Daniel turns and bumps into someone – a mother with a boy – she looks weirdly, suspiciously like Claudia Schiffer, though obviously it isn't her (though, in fact, it is). She's a very independent London mum.

CAROL: Sorry.

DANIEL: That's okay. My fault.

CAROL: No, really, it wasn't. You're Sam's dad, aren't you?

DANIEL: Yes. Stepdad, actually. Daniel.

CAROL: I'm Carol.

DANIEL: Carol?

Deep pause. The two adults just look at each other.

SAM: Okay, I'm back – let's go.

DANIEL: Yes – well – I hope we'll meet again, Karen.

CAROL: Carol. I'll make sure we do.

DANIEL: Yes. Good.

As they walk away …

SAM: Tell her.

DANIEL: What?

SAM: You know …

He starts making kissing noises.

DANIEL: Don't be such an arse.

136 EXT. SCHOOL – CAR PARK. NIGHT.

Lots of cars and action.

SAM: Look, there she is.

DANIEL: Where?

SAM: Over there.

Twenty yards away, Joanna gets into a big car – which instantly drives away.

SAM: Oh no.

DANIEL: Don't panic, we'll go to the airport. I know a short cut.

They get into their car and zoom off.

137 EXT. MARSEILLES. NIGHT.

Jamie arrives in a cab in a very thin, hilly and poor city street in Marseilles. He gets out of the cab, heads down and knocks on a door.

A man answers – about sixty – big belly – just wearing a vest. Jamie speaks in not quite fluent Portuguese. (All spoken Portuguese appears in italics.)

JAMIE: *Boa noite, Mr Barros – I am here to ask your daughter for her hands in marriage.*

MR BARROS: *You want to marry my daughter?*

JAMIE: *Yes.*

Mr Barros calls back into the house.

MR BARROS: *Come here – there is a man at the door.*

Through the plastic curtain leading into the next room comes a very big Portuguese girl. There's no love lost between father and daughter.

MR BARROS: *He wants to marry you.*

SOPHIA: *But I've never met him before.*

MR BARROS: *Who cares?*

SOPHIA: *You're going to sell me to a complete stranger?*

MR BARROS: *Sell? Who said 'sell'? I'll pay him.*

JAMIE: *Pardon me. I'm meaning your other daughter – Aurelia.*

MR BARROS: *She is not here. She's at work. I'll take you. You – stay here!*

SOPHIA: *As if I would. Stupid!*

The four of them, including a curious, old lady neighbour, head off down the steps – instantly passing a small restaurant where a few people are having supper outside.

SOPHIA: *Father is about to sell Aurelia as a slave to this Englishman.*

The people get up from their tables and follow. They don't want to miss this.

138 INT. HEATHROW AIRPORT – DEPARTURES. NIGHT.

Heathrow Airport – Daniel and Sam are rushing in. They look up at a board that says 'New York – Gate 36 – last call.'

DANIEL: Oh, no.

139 EXT. MARSEILLES. NIGHT.

Jamie and father and sister are moving through the streets followed by an ever-increasing crowd.

SOPHIA: *You better not say 'yes', father.*

MR BARROS: *Shut up, Miss Dunkin' Donut 2003.*

140 INT. HEATHROW AIRPORT – DEPARTURES. NIGHT.

Daniel and Sam reach the fast-track entry point.

DANIEL: Look, we're not actually flying.

GATE MAN: You can't come through without a boarding pass.

DANIEL: Not even to let the boy say goodbye to the love of his life?

GATE MAN: No.

DANIEL: I'm sorry, Sam.

Another passenger comes past.

GATE MAN: Boarding pass, sir.

The man is in great confusion.

ODD PASSENGER: Just give me a moment. I know I've got it here – if you'd just –
could you hold that for a second. (*Hands Gate Man his coat and hand luggage*)
There we go – now – it's – if you could just hang on to this . . .

DANIEL: Unless – you want to make a run for it.

SAM: Do you think I should?

*The Odd Passenger is Rufus from Selfridges. The Gate Man now has a large handcase
and a coat over his arms. Sam spots his chance. He makes a run for it – he charges
through, past the Gate Man – who doesn't see him go . . .*

ODD PASSENGER: I must have left it when I was having a cup of coffee. I'm sorry.

Rufus walks past Daniel.

141 INT. HEATHROW AIRPORT – DEPARTURES. NIGHT.

Meantime on the other side, Sam finds himself in the queue for security. He can't wait. He runs at the rectangular security machine, jumps over the security man at that moment kneeling to check a man's trousers.

Another security guard tries to catch him but is left holding nothing but his coat.

Sam is now in the main shopping area – airside – he sprints through it, hotly pursued by two security guards. Then he's running through a large empty corridor next to a moving walkway – by this time four guards are after him. He turns a corner and runs straight into a huge crowd of passengers with suitcases and dodges nimbly between them. The guards following are unable to move at quite the same speed and are slowed down by this obstacle.

He races through a blue door and finds he's emerged on to a level above the main concourse – finally he spots the sign saying 'Gate 36'. He looks down and sees Joanna and her family handing in their boarding cards.

142 EXT. MARSEILLES. NIGHT.

Now forty people are coming down a thinner set of steps – they reach the bottom, and turn sharp left, to head towards the restaurant.

CHILD 1:   *Apparently he is going to kill Aurelia.*

CHILD 2:   *Cool!*

143 INT. HEATHROW AIRPORT – DEPARTURES GATE. NIGHT.

Sam finally reaches the doors of the room that is Gate 36 – and can see Joanna just going through to the plane …

But a sturdy security guard and a couple of hostesses stand between him and her. He's stumped – till suddenly they turn – noticing that up on the television screens along the side of the room, Billy is starting to take his clothes off as he performs his song. He is playing 'Christmas Is All Around', increasingly naked.

Sam takes his chance and nips in.

SAM: Joanna.

JOANNA: Sam?

SAM: I thought you didn't know my name.

JOANNA: Course I do.

Now all his pursuers have arrived.

SAM: Jesus. I've got to run.

144 INT. HEATHROW AIRPORT – DEPARTURES. NIGHT.

We cut to Sam, being led out by guards towards a waiting Daniel.

As he moves towards Daniel with a smile on his face, he does the big 'one' gesture – and suddenly gets a tap on his shoulder. He turns – it's Joanna – she kisses him on the cheek. Then she turns and runs back.

Sam grins like a madman and runs to Daniel, who lifts him in the air and spins him round, father and son, together.

145 EXT. MARSEILLES. NIGHT.

We see a tide of sixty people sweeping down an alley – they've been collecting at Sophia's instigation.

Suddenly they have arrived at a humble Portuguese restaurant. Jamie hesitates before entering – but then heads on in.

146 INT. MARSEILLES RESTAURANT. NIGHT.

There is a proprietor with a huge black moustache behind the bar.

MR BARROS: *Where is Aurelia?*

PROPRIETOR: *Why should I tell you?*

MR BARROS: *This man wants to marry her.*

PROPRIETOR: *He can't do that – she's our best waitress.*

And at that moment Aurelia appears upstairs holding plates of food – she turns and sees Jamie standing there. She freezes. And then very gently puts the food down. She's probably wearing make-up for the first time in the film.

JAMIE: *Boa noite, Aurelia.*

AURELIA: *Boa noite, Jamie.*

Pause. The entire restaurant has fallen silent and is listening.

JAMIE: *Beautiful Aurelia – I've come here with a view to asking you . . . to marriage me.*

Cut to her.

I know I seems an insane person – because I hardly knows you – but sometimes things are so transparency, they don't need evidential proof. And I will inhabit here, or you can inhabit with me in England.

SOPHIA: *Definitely go for England, girl. You'll meet Prince William – then you can marry him instead.*

MR BARROS: *Ssssh.*

JAMIE: *Of course I don't expecting you to be as foolish as me, and of course I prediction you say 'no' – but it's Christmas and I just wanted to . . . check.*

Pause as she thinks.

SOPHIA: *Oh God, say 'yes', you skinny moron.*

Cut back to Aurelia and back to Jamie. Then – because she too has learnt the language of the person she loves, in very broken English.

AURELIA: Thank you – that will be nice. 'Yes' is being my answer . . . Easy question.

MR BARROS: *What did you say?*

AURELIA: *Yes, of course.*

Everyone cheers and applauds. She heads down the tiny sweeping staircase. The band starts to play.

JAMIE: You learnt English?

AURELIA: Just in cases.

Aurelia and Jamie move together and kiss. They are interrupted by a tap on his shoulder — Aurelia's sister plants a huge kiss on his mouth. A second later her father does exactly the same.

147 INT. HEATHROW AIRPORT – ARRIVALS GATE. DAY.

It is one month later.

The arrivals gate opens to reveal Billy – he has a gorgeous six-foot blonde with him. Joe steps out of the crowd to meet them.

JOE: Hello, Daisy.

BILLY: This one's Greta.

JOE: Hello, Greta.

Next out are Jamie and the radiant Aurelia. Peter and Juliet are there to greet him.

JAMIE: Well, here she is – this is Aurelia. This is Juliet, Peter…
Oh, Mark, hi – I didn't see you.

For indeed, he is there, hanging behind.

MARK: Yeah, just thought I'd tag along.

AURELIA: Jamie's friends are so good-looking. He never tells me this. I think maybe now I make the wrong choice – pick the wrong Englishman.

JAMIE: She can't speak English properly. She doesn't know what she's saying.

Harry comes out and looks around – seems to be no one there – but actually Karen is waiting, smiling, dutiful. And there are the kids carrying a sign – 'Welcome Home Dad'. Harry hesitantly goes to kiss Karen. She lets him. She is trying to mend things…

HARRY: How are you?

KAREN: I'm fine. I'm fine. (*With reserve*) Good to have you back.
Come on – home.

Then it is Joanna, the little girl – cut to Daniel and Sam waiting – and Carol, with the cups of coffee she's just bought.

SAM: There she is.

Sam breaks through, runs to her – then realizes he has to hold back.

JOANNA: Hi.

SAM: Hello.

DANIEL: He should have
kissed her.

CAROL: No, that's cool.

*Tony is also waiting – he's
tapped on the shoulder –
there with huge grins are
John and Judy.*

TONY: Hey! What are you
two doing here?

*She wiggles an engagement
ring on her finger. They
couldn't be happier.*

JOHN: I might get a shag at last.

JUDY: Naughty.

JOHN: Gotta go.

JUDY: Bye!

Tony turns back as the arrivals gate opens to reveal Colin, waving and whooping triumphantly.

COLIN: This is Harriet.

He turns and points behind him – and through the doors comes his new girlfriend. She is staggeringly beautiful. She is Harriet.

HARRIET: Hi – really pleased to meet you.

TONY: Hello, Harriet.

HARRIET: I sort of brought my sister to stay … this is Carla. She's real friendly.

And Harriet gestures backwards – coming through the customs is the fifth staggering and gorgeous American woman.

CARLA: Hello, you must be Tony.

She hugs him and then kisses him full on the lips.

I heard you were gorgeous.

She kisses him again. Tony is stunned. But not in a bad way.

Then cameras start to flash – a big stir and the PM comes through, surrounded by security people. Natalie rushes through the crowd and hugs him with total love, throwing her legs round his waist – flashes of thirty waiting paparazzi flash.

PM: God, you weigh a lot.

NATALIE: Oh shut your face.

They walk off happily together. We move to genuine footage of real people hugging and kissing friends and family from across the world. We're back in the world of normal people – with love actually . . . all around.

THE END

'Christmas Is All Around'
The Lyrics

Written by **Reg Presley**
Adapted by **Santa Claus**
Performed by **Billy Mack**

I feel it in my fingers,
I feel it in my toes,
Christmas Is All Around me
And so the feeling grows.
It's written on the wind,
It's everywhere I go,
So if you really love Christmas
Come on and let it snow.

You know I love Christmas, I always will
My mind's made up by the way that I feel
There's no beginning, there'll be no end
'Cause on Christmas you can depend.

I see Santa before me,
As I lay on my bed,
I kind of get to thinking
Of all the things you said.
You gave your presents to me,
And I gave mine to you,
I need someone beside me
In everything I do.

You know I love Christmas, I always will
My mind's made up by the way that I feel
There's no beginning, there'll be no end
'Cause on Christmas you can depend.

I see Santa before me
As I lay on my bed
I kind of get to thinking
Of all the things you said.

You know I love Christmas, I always will
My mind's made up by the way that I feel
There's no beginning, there'll be no end
'Cause on Christmas you can depend.

It's written on the wind,
It's everywhere I go,
So if you really love Christmas
Come on and let it show
Come on and let it show
So if you really love Christmas
Come on and let it show
So if you really love Christmas
Come on and let it show.

Deleted Scenes
The Ones That Didn't Make It

The process of writing and making this film has been a long one – always is – and the amount of stuff written and left behind far exceeds the amount of stuff there is left in the movie. I remember working out that on *Notting Hill* for every day I worked on the film (I tend to write about twenty pages a day) there were twelve seconds in the finished film (that's about a fifth of a page).

These are a few selected scenes from some different stages of the film. First – a character called Martin, who eventually disappeared completely. He was a friend of Daniel, Liam Neeson's character, and we join him and some other friends in a pub a few weeks after the death of Daniel's wife. Except, at that point, I was just calling Liam's character Sad Dad.

THE FUNERAL FANTASY

MARTIN: Right – it's how long since Katie died?

We come upon three, forty-something guys and one woman of that age, in a bar – just chatting after work …

SAD DAD: Five months.

MARTIN: Is that long enough to be tactless?

SAD DAD: I think so. Forgive me if it turns out not.

MARTIN: Absolutely. The thing is this – I just want to check … about the funeral fantasy.

SAD DAD: What's that?

MARTIN: The funeral fantasy – come on, every married man has had it.

JULIAN: I'm married, I haven't had it.

MARTIN: Are you sure?

JULIAN: Yes – what is it?

MARTIN: Okay – maybe it's just me, in which case I'm deeply ashamed. The funeral fantasy is the one where you imagine that your wife dies – it's terrible, it's tragic. When you're thinking about it, you always feel a tear threatening to trickle – and then it's the funeral…

We see all of this as he describes it …

… and all the family are at the back – and in your area, the crowd seems to consist mainly of your now dead wife's foxiest friends. Also every girl you ever fancied, all of whom have come along to be supportive, all dressed in these very tight black little suits – with very fetishy veils and lots of leg – and it's quite a cold day and they cry a lot and when it's over, as you walk back, this desperately cute friend of your wife in a tiny black skirt comes up and says…

We see her mouth say this, though it's still Martin's voice speaking.

…'Martin – if you're lonely, you know – I'm there for you. I know it wouldn't mean anything, it would just be comfort – but I'd do it, for her…' And then at the reception this just keeps happening – and by the end of the party, you've got someone sorted for every day of the week and so, for the next month, you're having sex with a different, totally undemanding girl daily and at the end of the month, you just pick one of them and your conscience is clear because she's your wife's friend and it's difficult for both of you, but…

Cut to a naked woman lying on a bed – again, her mouth says this, with Martin's voice…

'It would have made her very happy.'

Cut back to the table – they're open-mouthed at the story.

JULIAN: Yeah, on second thoughts, I have had that one.

GEORGE: Yup, me too.

KATHY: Me too.

MARTIN: Girls have it too?

KATHY: Absolutely – men look so sexy in those black funeral suits.

MARTIN: So, my question is – part one and part two – first, when it actually happens, the tragic death, does the funeral fantasy even occur to you? And second – does it actually happen, and during the first month after Kate died, did you spend the entire time in comforting sex with a variety of her more attractive friends, in which number I would obviously and proudly include my ex-wife?

SAD DAD: Well, I hate to disappoint you, but – when it actually happens, it is unfortunately so awful that your brain doesn't go that way…

MARTIN: Damn.

SAD DAD: And then at the funeral the only people who demand physical intimacy are very large maiden aunts. It's a day for kissing women with moustaches.

MARTIN: Right. Right. Disappointing. Very disappointing.

Then something genuinely occurs to him.

SAD DAD: Though, actually, come to think of it – the mother of one of Sam's friends was very… oddly dressed that day… I think her name is Yolanda… I mean, this was a real micro skirt.

We see Yolanda in slo-mo from his wife's funeral. She certainly looks pretty great, tight black suit and wind-blown hair.

MARTIN: Yes!!! YES!!! YES ! She's the one! It happens! We can dream on, boys – when the worst happens, the best does indeed happen. Come on – champagne all round.

JULIAN: How is Sam? Is he okay?

SAD DAD: Ahm – no – not great – in fact, I'm getting a bit worried actually. He's getting very strange and I just can't get through.

MARTIN: Oh sod him. He's probably just a little weird creep, mother dead or alive, like my kid – he'll sort himself out, don't you worry. Drink up.

SAD DAD: I hope so.

While we're on Daniel – here's a little section with him and Sam that came and went. By this time, his character had changed from Sad Dad to just Dad. This scene came just after Sam admitted he was in love.

BOY'S TALK

Knock on the door. Enter Dad…

DAD: Okay – let's review the situation. Option one – ask her out.

SAM: Impossible.

DAD: Fair enough – option two – this is a very cunning one – become… her… friend.

SAM: She's the most popular girl in the school and she hates boys.

DAD: Right. Option three – kidnap her and keep her tied up in your room until she agrees to marry you ...

SAM: It's a route I've considered.

DAD: Right, and quite rightly rejected on the grounds of...

SAM: Hygiene.

DAD: Exactly. Okay – I'll keep thinking ... *(Exits and comes straight back in again)* It could be worse, you know – after all, you must have at least one chance in a thousand – she's in your school – you can at least talk to her.

Sam just shakes his head.

It's a distinctly better position than me and Claudia Schiffer.

SAM: You're in love with Claudia Schiffer?

DAD: Always was – for the last five years of her life, your mother always knew she was number two in my affections.

SAM: You should look her up on the net.

DAD: Can you do that?

SAM: Yes – just go to Yahoo or Excite and type in 'Claudia Schiffer'.

DAD: Cool. Who's your favourite movie star?

SAM: Don't like any of them. My heart lies elsewhere.

DAD: Wow. A one-woman man.

SAM: Yup. A one-girl boy.

This led on to a section which we actually did film but isn't in the movie – though it'll be on the DVD. Why did we cut it? In the end, the funeral and sorrow side of Daniel felt so strong at the start that the Claudia Schiffer internet thing seemed a touch tactless. And the cut from Daniel worrying about Sam with Karen in the kitchen to him and lonely Sam sitting on a bench by the Thames and discussing his problems seemed so strong the first time we did it, that everything in between was doomed.

In the set-up in the film, Sam and Daniel weren't actually talking at this point – it was Emma Thompson's character who had mentioned Claudia Schiffer's website – so the point of this scene was at last to break down the barrier of non-communication between Sam and his dad.

THE TROUBLE WITH CLAUDIA

INT. DANIEL'S HOUSE – CORRIDOR/OFFICE. DAY.

It's a Saturday morning. Daniel walks past Sam's room – it's locked – there's strange music coming from in there ...

He walks past, shaking his head, and heads down into his office. He sits down and pushes a button – the computer starts up – a boring work spreadsheet ... he's bored.

He types in 'Excite' – then 'Claudia Schiffer'. Instantly up comes a list of ten Claudia Schiffer-based sites. The fourth one says 'Claudia Schiffer Naked Naked Naked'.

Daniel goes to it – there's a seductive picture of Claudia, and a list of photos – gallery 1, gallery 2, etc. He opens one – and up come tiny pictures of Claudia, many not fully clothed. He double clicks on one of them – but it doesn't come up – instead, there's a form that says he can't go any further without giving a credit-card number.

So he closes it. But when he does, lots of pictures of naked girls come up uninvited. It's a site called 'XXXX Teen Sluts'.

At which moment Daniel hears a car pulling up outside. He swiftly closes 'XXXX Teen Sluts' – but other things come up, increasingly pornographic and always with the words 'come' or 'pink' in their title. He tries to close them, but more and more boxes start coming up – and finally the machine freezes – a patchwork of breasts and bottoms of all shapes and sizes. And there seems to be a donkey in there.

The doorbell goes.

And now Daniel can't move the cursor to get the damn thing to shut down … He goes to the plug to turn off the electricity – but it doesn't make any difference. In desperation, he takes off his jumper and throws it over the quite big computer screen.

INT. DANIEL'S FRONT DOOR. DAY.

Cut to Daniel at the front door. It's his father-in-law – a very respectable, bespectacled man.

DANIEL: Hello, Matthew.

They shake hands – and then awkwardly drift into a hug. At this moment, both can only think of wife, of daughter.

FATHER-IN-LAW: Still a bit hard, isn't it?

DANIEL: Still a little tricky. Come and sit down.

FATHER-IN-LAW: Why not? I've brought a little gift for my grandson – thanks to him, I've actually started to use that computer you gave me.

DANIEL: Really?

FATHER-IN-LAW: Yes, I've found a tremendous golfing site. In fact, let me show you – where's your computer?

DANIEL: Ahm – let's have a cup of coffee first, shall we?

FATHER-IN-LAW: No, I insist – come on – in the office, I presume.

Father-in-law heads into the office. He takes the jumper off the machine, the screen is black – he pushes a button and up flicks the pornographic patchwork. He looks up at Daniel – Daniel at him. Pause.

DANIEL: Oh … this is disgusting. Where's Sam? This is just a step too far…

He runs up the steps to Sam's room – knocks on the door – Sam peeks his head out.

DANIEL: Do you want fifty pounds – yes or no?

SAM: I'd prefer a hundred.

DANIEL: Okay, then whatever happens in the next minute – don't argue – just agree with me. On everything.

SAM: Okay.

DANIEL: Right. (*Raising voice*) Get down here young man, straight away.

INT. DANIEL'S HOUSE – OFFICE. DAY.

Cut to the three of them in the office.

DANIEL: What is this, young sir?

SAM: I don't know – looks like a website about women having sex with animals.

DANIEL: And how did it get here?

Pause. Daniel realizes that was too complex.

All right. I'll tell you how it got here. You've been using my computer, Sam, and calling up this filth – haven't you?

He looks at him with slightly raised eyebrows.

SAM: Yes, I have.

DANIEL: I don't know what to say. I hope you're ashamed of yourself.

SAM: Yes, I am.

DANIEL: It's disgusting, isn't it?

SAM: It really is.

FATHER-IN-LAW: Don't worry – we all have different ways of coping with grief and maybe, Sam, this is yours – let's just forget about it.

DANIEL: I can't forget about it. I am so angry with you, Sam – that is your pocket money docked for a month, young man.

EXT. BANK CASH MACHINE. DAY.

Cut to three hours later – a cash machine somewhere near the river – out pops £100 and Daniel puts it straight into Sam's hand.

DANIEL: Brilliant work, son.

EXT. MILLENNIUM BRIDGE. DAY.

They are walking home across the Millennium Bridge.

SAM: Only one thing I don't understand – why were you looking up women having sex with animals?

DANIEL: I wasn't – I was doing some work, and ... looking up Claudia Schiffer – for work reasons – and then suddenly, when I tried to close the damn thing, that stuff came up.

SAM: You must have been looking up 'Claudia Schiffer Naked'.

DANIEL: No.

SAM: You must have – it's number 4 on the 'Claudia Schiffer list – Claudia Schiffer Naked Naked Naked' – if you just looked up the Claudia Schiffer homepage it wouldn't have done that.

Pause. Then fast...

DANIEL: All right, I was looking up 'Claudia Schiffer Naked Naked Naked', you little greedy bastard.

He starts to laugh.

SAM: Pervert.

DANIEL: Computer nerd.

SAM: Wanky, wanky weirdo.

DANIEL: Freak with genuinely bad haircut.

They're now laughing a lot – friends together at last. Maybe their first laugh since Sam's mum died.

And it was after that that they sat on the bench and discussed the real, extra reason for Sam's sorrow – the love thing.

Next up, another scene we filmed with Sarah and her brother. Once again, when we finally cut the film, less was more – but here we went a little deeper into their relationship, with an extraordinary performance by Michael Fitzgerald, who was also in our film *The Tall Guy*.

SISTER AND BROTHER

INT. HOSPITAL. NIGHT.

Sarah is in the ward with her brother again.

SARAH: Do you remember Dad and the Christmas pudding?

MICHAEL: No.

SARAH: Every year Mum served it up – said it was a great English tradition. Every year he never took a single bite.

He just looks at her. Nothing. Then…

MICHAEL: You used to clear the table for the only time during the whole year because the Christmas *Top of the Pops* was on and you could watch it in the kitchen.

Deep inside, he remembers everything – she takes his lead. It's such a joy when he talks.

SARAH: That's right. Couldn't wash up enough. Washing up my absolute favourite activity for one meal a year.

He just looks at her stonily. Then a tiny smile.

I've just realized – Mum was a terrible cook, wasn't she?

MICHAEL: Yes. She was. Remember – egg in a cup.

He thinks. Looks at her. Another tiny smile.

How are you, Blondie?

SARAH: Great. Everything's great.

Its not true. He nods. He's pleased.

MICHAEL: Great. I'm in hell.

SARAH: I know you are. I know you are, babe.

She takes his hand.

SARAH: Love you, Michael.

MICHAEL: I know…Doesn't help.

SARAH: I know.

And finally, something I wish I had been able to make work. We went all the way to Kenya to film this. The point, right near the end of the film, was to show that love is a factor everywhere in the world – even in the most extreme circumstances. But in the end, we were juggling so many balls at this point of the film, that we had to drop this one.

THE AFRICAN POSTER

EXT/INT. FAIRTRADE OFFICE. NIGHT.

Slightly mysterious midnight mood. We drift across the office and come to the African poster behind Sarah's desk. It is of two very old African women, carrying huge bundles of sticks on their backs. We slowly move into it…

EXT. AFRICA. DAY.

The women begin to talk. But their conversation, instead of being about their hard lives, is just about life and family and gossip. And love.

OLD WOMAN 1: But he's a famous fool.

OLD WOMAN 2: I know – but my daughter loves him – so what can I do?

OLD WOMAN 1: Tell her that if she marries him, you'll disown her and never see either of them again.

OLD WOMAN 2: Yes – I could do that. Or tell her that her father was also a famous fool – and he didn't turn out too badly.

OLD WOMAN 1: You're right – you married a real idiot.

They both laugh.

OLD WOMAN 2: Didn't we all? (*More laughter*) How is Tessefaye?

OLD WOMAN 1: Terrible. Gorgeous – but a terrible man.

Behind every film ever made is another film… deleted.

Behind the Scenes

The next few pages show a few of the shots Peter Mountain took behind the scenes during our shoot. The people you glimpse in them are the people who really made the film – actors come and go – directors head back to their trailers for doughnuts – it's the other people who work really, really hard. Most of the time . . .

I remember Mike Newell, who directed *Four Weddings*, saying, 'In the end, it's actually got to happen on camera – the thing has to really occur'. And that's the miracle of actors: after all that preparation – and in front of all those people – the actors just have to live the completely real moment or the audience will spot the fakery. Confronted by cameras, buffed and polished by costume, hair and make-up, fussed over by props, given stupid notes by directors, from somewhere they still manage to conjure up real life.

Hugh dancing was one of the very interesting sections of filming. We suddenly
had very, very little time left and it was our last day with Hugh. We got off to a brave
start, but Hugh made the mistake of coming to the monitor to watch the play back.
'Is that what I really looked like? I'm completely out of time.' But he pressed on
bravely. The next set-up he had another look. With some sorrow, and a little nostalgia,
he whispered, 'I will never dance in public again.' So what you see in the
movie is not only the first time Hugh Grant ever danced on film. It also may be
the last time he'll ever dance, full stop.

The man in the blue shirt tells the horrified actors about the animal life he has just found in the lake.

One of the actors starts to become intimately acquainted with the lake's idiosyncratic and infectious wildlife.

The same actor shows the director how she feels when he asks her if she'd mind having another go at shooting the sequence in the lake.

This picture is by Charlie Mackesy as are the other lovely, mysterious drawings in this book. He was our own private artist and it was a joy to have him around, pen and camera in hand. And, in fact, in the film itself, when Colin Firth and his brother turn in the direction of Colin's girlfriend at the end of that early scene, there is a picture of an angel by Charlie in between them.

Richard Rowan + Liam.

This is Peter Taylor's private page – our extraordinary camera operator. That's the back of his head on the left and the front of it on the right.

Love Actually
The Quiz

You've seen the film, you've read the script – but were you actually paying attention? Try this quiz to find out – and remember that it is very immature to cheat (though, even cheating comes in all different shapes and sizes. If, for instance, you go back to the script to seek out the answers, that might just be called research. On the other hand, if you go to the next page and just read the answers there, that really is cheating and you should pay more attention to the teachings of Jesus, who was born at Christmas, when the film is set).

QUESTIONS

1. How long has Sarah been working for Harry exactly?
   (one point for each detail)

2. What is Jamie's surname?

3. What is Natalie's octopus brother called?

4. What does Colin think the food at the reception tastes like?

5. Which Radio Station is Billy interviewed on?

6. Which sexual positions do we see John and Judy in?
   (one point for each)

7. Where does Natalie tell the PM she lives? (one point for each detail)

8. What is Karen and Harry's son called?

9. What is Colin's surname?

10. Which carol does the PM sing to the three little girls?

11. What is Billy's message to the kids about drugs?

12. What kind of book is Jamie writing?

13. Where does Colin say he's from to the girls in the bar?

14. How much does Harry pay for the necklace?

15. Which ambassador does the PM want to change the meeting
    with after his secretary catches him dancing?

16. What is written on Sam's door when he's practising the drums
    in his room?

17. Who should people avoid at the Christmas party 'if they want their
    breasts unfondled'?

18. What is Mark watching on TV when Juliet turns up at his house?

19. What is the name of Harriet's 'real friendly' sister?

20. What are the seven things the PM says make Britain great?
    (one point for each)

    Don't worry if you do badly – Richard Curtis scored 24/36, and
    he wrote the film, directed it and then edited it for six months. In fact,
    if you score more than 24, it's going to be slightly worrying . . .

ANSWERS

1. 2 years, 7 months, 3 days and 2 hours.
2. Bennett.
3. Keith.
4. A dead baby's finger.
5. Radio Watford.
6. (a) From behind (b) Judy on top (c) You know perfectly well
(d) Judy sits on John's face – or quite near it.
7. (a) Wandsworth (b) The dodgy end (c) Harris Street
(d) At the end of the High Street (e) Near the Queen's Head.
8. Bernard.
9. Frissell.
10. 'Good King Wenceslas'.
11. 'Don't buy drugs. Become a pop star and they give you them for free'.
12. A thriller.
13. Basildon.
14. £270.
15. Japanese.
16. Ringo Rules or Rhythm is My Life.
17. Kevin.
18. Billy's video.
19. Carla.
20. (a) Shakespeare (b) Churchill (c) The Beatles (d) Sean Connery (e) Harry Potter
(f) David Beckham's right foot (g) David Beckham's left foot. The original script also
included 'both Catherine Zeta-Jones's breasts' but Hugh found, quite rightly, that he
couldn't say it with any credibility in the context of a Prime Ministerial press conference.

THE SCORE
How did you do? Tell the truth.

24–36 Oh, come on – don't pretend you didn't look SOME of the answers up.
If not, then full marks for your powers of observation. Are you Sherlock Holmes?
No you can't be – he's not a real detective.

12–24 Definitely not the class swot, but not bad.

0–12 Are you sure you've seen Love Actually?

Love Questionnaire
Abdul Salis (TONY)

Who was the first person you ever loved –
and how old were they and you?
Kelly Graham – I'm sure I loved her or Tammy
Cope. We were seven or eight. I went out with
Kelly Graham for two years. Vicki Barker was
nice but she was younger than me.

Who was the first person you loved in the movies?
Claire Danes in *My So-Called Life* (actually that
was TV) – and I wished I was Jared Leto.

What is your favourite romantic movie of all time?
Notting Hill, *Cocktail* – and *Footloose!* Actually,
Lori Singer was the first girl I fell in love with.

What is your favourite romantic song?
'From The Heart' – Another Level.

What's your favourite Christmas song?
The Simpsons, 'Christmas Boogie' – I sing
it every Christmas.

What is your best ever Christmas present?
A Knight Rider radio-control car. Hands down.
Although I broke it on Christmas Day.

And what is your worst?
My sister got me a beard trimmer. I have never
had a beard.

If you had to have sex with one British
Prime Minister, who would it be?
I've even thought about this before being asked.
It's got to be the Iron Lady.

Who would you have as your naked stand-in?
Denzel Washington, Lenny Kravitz or Vas
Blackwood.

Is love actually all around?
Love Actually is All Around. Most definitely.

Love Questionnaire
Alan Rickman (HARRY)

Who was the first person you ever loved – and how old were they and you?
Amanda. From afar. We were ten. At sports day, blonde hair flying, she won the 100 yards by a mile.

Who was the first person you loved in the movies?
Jeanne Moreau. And Jules. And Jim.

What is your favourite romantic movie of all time?
The Philadelphia Story.

What is your favourite romantic song?
'Take It With Me' by Tom Waits.

What's your favourite Christmas song?
'Merry Christmas' by John Lennon.

What is your best ever Christmas present?
A box containing a shiny half-crown and three handkerchiefs with 'A' in the corner.

And what is your worst?
A scratched coffee grinder with no box and oily thumbprints. You know who you are.

If you had to have sex with one British Prime Minister, who would it be?
You must be joking.

Who would you have as your naked stand-in?
Liam Neeson's choice. Or Liam Neeson. Or almost anyone, at this point.

Is love actually all around?
Actually, yes. In spite of all the shite.

Love Questionnaire
Andrew Lincoln (MARK)

Who was the first person you ever loved – and how old were they and you?
Sarah Bennett (famous for her burgundy legwarmers). She was ten and
I was nine.

Who was the first person you loved in the movies?
Fenella Fielding, who played Valeria the vampire in *Carry On Screaming.*

What is your favourite romantic movie of all time?
Some Like It Hot.

What is your favourite romantic song?
'Hallelujah' by Jeff Buckley.

What's your favourite Christmas song?
'Power of Love' by Frankie Goes to Hollywood.

What is your best ever Christmas present?
My dog Charlie – now deceased.

And what is your worst?
A £5 gift voucher for WH Smith.

If you had to have sex with one British Prime Minister, who would it be?
Winston Churchill.

Who would you have as your naked stand-in?
Bill Nighy.

Is love actually all around?
Yeah, baby, yeah!

Love Questionnaire
Bill Nighy
(BILLY)

Who was the first person you ever loved – and how old were they and you?
Riff the dog – I was nine and the dog was about six weeks.

Who was the first person you loved in the movies?
Peggy Ashcroft or Celia Johnson.

What is your favourite romantic movie of all time?
The Hairdresser's Husband or *Romauld et Juliette*.

What is your favourite romantic song?
'Love Minus Zero' or 'She Belongs to Me' – both by Bob Dylan.

What's your favourite Christmas song?
'Run Run Rudolph (Santa's Got To Make It To Town)' by Chuck Berry.

What is your best ever Christmas present?
A short story from my daughter.

And what is your worst?
A tie with ponies and crossed riding crops on it.

If you had to have sex with one British Prime Minister, who would it be?
Harold Wilson by a mile.

Who would you have as your naked stand-in?
Keith Richard.

Is love actually all around?
Yeah yeah yeah.

Love Questionnaire
Chiwetel Ejiofor
(PETER)

Who was the first person you ever loved –
and how old were they and you?
I was probably zero and she was in her early
twenties – my Mum.

Who was the first person you loved in the movies?
Teri Garr in *Tootsie*.

What is your favourite romantic movie of all time?
Manhattan.

What is your favourite romantic song?
'Something So Right' by Paul Simon.

What's your favourite Christmas song?
'It Feels Like Christmas' by The Muppets.

What is your best ever Christmas present?
It was a mini Steve Davis snooker table
when I was ten.

And what is your worst?
There's no such thing as a worst Christmas present.

If you had to have sex with one British Prime Minister,
who would it be?
That's really a tough question. I'd have to get to know
them really well. God forgive me – I guess it would have
to be Margaret Thatcher.

Who would you have as your naked stand-in?
Johnny Vegas.

Is love actually all around?
Of course it is.

Love Questionnaire
Colin Firth (JAMIE)

Who was the first person you ever loved – and how old were they and you?
It might be Heather Bailey – I was eight. There were crushes before then but she was the first person I cried over. Actually, no – I think it was Lynne Lassin. I loved her because she loved me. Well, not JUST because she loved me – but, you know, it helped.

Who is your favourite romantic poem?
'Every Day You Play' by Pablo Neruda.

What is your favourite romantic movie of all time?
I'm afraid I'm not really a massive fan of romantic films. I like feeling a bit upset at a movie ending, rather than warm and fuzzy – I mean I prefer *Brief Encounter* to *Sleepless in Seattle*.

What is your favourite romantic song?
'Hot Baritto Number 1' by Gram Parsons.

What's your favourite Christmas song?
'Fairy Tale of New York' by The Pogues.

What is your best ever Christmas present?
A plastic sword. I was six.

And what is your worst?
The plastic sword – my brother, who was a toddler, got past the fireguard with it on Christmas Day and then walked round the house with this burning brazier dropping molten plastic on to the linoleum tiles in the hall and the living room carpet. It was nearly the death of my entire family, but I just missed my lovely sword.

If you had to have sex with one British Prime Minister, who would it be?
Well I wouldn't have fucked Callaghan, that's for sure. Would I fuck Attlee? I don't know. I think Pitt the Younger sounds promising – at least he's not some jowly old incontinent. But it's so much easier with American presidents, isn't it.

Who would you have as your naked stand-in?
Hugh Grant ten years ago.

Is love actually all around?
Pass.

Love Questionnaire
Emma Thompson
(KAREN)

Who was the first person you ever loved – and how
old were they and you?
Matthew Fox at primary school. He was six-ish and I fell
in love when he kissed me while we were both hanging
upside down on a clothes-rail during the school play.
We were dressed as rabbits.

Who was the first person you loved in the movies?
Buster Keaton.

What is your favourite romantic movie of all time?
Les Enfants du Paradis / Some Like It Hot.

What is your favourite romantic song?
'Without You' by Harry Nilsson.

What's your favourite Christmas song?
'Merry Christmas Everyone' by Slade.

What is your best ever Christmas present?
My first stocking when I was two. I never got over it.

And what is your worst?
A half-eaten MilkyWay rewrapped and sent by
my Aunt Mill. She wasn't well.

If you had to have sex with one British Prime Minister,
who would it be?
Winston Churchill. I mean, imagine the pillow-talk.

Who would you have as your naked stand-in?
Cameron Diaz.

Is love actually all around?
YES.

Love Questionnaire
Gregor Fisher (JOE)

Who was the first person you ever loved – and how old were they and you?
Patricia Smith. I was eight and so was she. She wasn't a blind bit interested.

Who was the first person you loved in the movies?
The Swiss Family Robinson – the entire family (especially the large Great Dane).

What is your favourite romantic movie of all time?
Summer of '42.

What is your favourite romantic song?
'The Rose' by Bette Midler.

What's your favourite Christmas song?
'Silent Night'.

What is your best ever Christmas present?
My son Alexander getting into university.

And what is your worst?
I don't have one!

If you had to have sex with one British Prime Minister, who would it be?
It would have to be Churchill. He'd be so pissed he probably wouldn't be able to do anything, so you'd be perfectly safe.

Who would you have as your naked stand-in?
Jamie Lee Curtis.

Is love actually all around?
Yes – but you've just got to look for it.

Love Questionnaire
Heike Makatsch (MIA)

Who was the first person you ever loved – and how old were they and you?
Patrick Bonecker, son of a befriended family. We were about six and
discovered a lot.

Who was the first person you loved in the movies?
Marilyn Monroe in *Some Like It Hot*. When she dances with the ukulele,
I fell for her.

What is your favourite romantic movie of all time?
Love Story. I cried cried cried and couldn't stop for hours afterwards.

What is your favourite romantic song?
'I Guess That's Why They Call It The Blues' by Elton John.

What's your favourite Christmas song?
'I Wish It Could Be Christmas Every Day' by Wizzard.

What is your best ever Christmas present?
My parents gave me a Lego train track set with all sorts of landscape design –
it worked on batteries.

And what is your worst?
See above. I hated it at the time because I actually had expected the newest
Barbie and accessories.

If you had to have sex with one British Prime Minister, who would it be?
Winston Churchill.

Who would you have as your naked stand-in?
Definitely Marlene Dietrich's legs.

Is love actually all around?
No, but it rules in my house.

Love Questionnaire
Hugh Grant (PM)

Who was the first person you ever loved – and how old were they and you?
A girl called Juliet. I was eleven. She was thirteen, blonde, wore glasses and looked a bit like the then Labour Party leader, Michael Foot.

What's your favourite romantic poem?
There's an enchanting limerick that begins 'There was a young girl called Heather'.

What is your favourite romantic movie of all time?
Brief Encounter. I could play that part.

What is your favourite romantic song?
'Daniel', as sung by my grandmother's Pekinese dog, Mee Too, who always joined in when this song came on.

What's your favourite Christmas song?
'Away In a Manger', as sung by my accountant, who likes to send audio Christmas cards.

What is your best ever Christmas present?
An air gun. I went straight out and shot a bee.

And what is your worst?
Set of iron-on jeans patches in plain denim.

If you had to have sex with one British Prime Minister, who would it be?
Michael Foot, for sentimental reasons (don't think he ever made it though).

Who would you have as your naked stand-in?
Colin Firth – but with a better body.

Is love actually all around?
No. The world is full of hatred and greed.

Love Questionnaire
Joanna Page (JUDY)

Who was the first person you ever loved – and how old were they and you?
Michael Honey when I was seven years old and so was he, but he dumped me for football.

Who was the first person you loved in the movies?
Robert Redford in his white sailor/officer's uniform!

What is your favourite romantic movie of all time?
The Way We Were.

What is your favourite romantic song?
'Evergreen' by Barbra Streisand, not Will Young.

What's your favourite Christmas song?
'I Wish It Could Be Christmas Every Day' by Wizzard.

What is your best ever Christmas present?
My engagement ring! (Delivered to me by my Jack Russell terrier!)

And what is your worst?
A packet of tissues.

If you had to have sex with one British Prime Minister, who would it be?
Winston Churchill – it would be memorable.

Who would you have as your naked stand-in?
Jessica Lange, as long as I could have her face and voice too!

Is love actually all around?
It is in South Wales!!

Love Questionnaire
Keira Knightley (JULIET)

Who was the first person you ever loved – and how
old were they and you?
Charlie Lewis – I was four and a half and he was four
and three quarters – an older man.

Who was the first person you loved in the movies?
Leonardo di Caprio in *Romeo & Juliet*.

What is your favourite romantic movie of all time?
A dead heat between *Casablanca* and *Now Voyager*.

What is your favourite romantic song?
'My Baby Just Cares For Me' by Nina Simone.

What's your favourite Christmas song?
'Rudolph the Red Nose Reindeer', of course.

What is your best ever Christmas present?
A Scalextric set – which I got last year!

And what is your worst?
So many millions of them. Lots and lots of bad jumpers.

If you had to have sex with one British Prime Minister,
who would it be?
That's an absolutely disgusting question –
they're all horrible. Maybe Lloyd George because
of the moustache.

Who would you have as your naked stand-in?
Johnny Depp.

Is love actually all around?
Yes, absolutely.

Love Questionnaire
Kris Marshall (COLIN)

Who was the first person you ever loved – and how old were they and you?
Myself – we were both five.

Who was the first person you loved in the movies?
Donald Pleasence in *The Great Escape* – but not in a gay way.
Either that or *Scooby Doo*.

What is your favourite romantic movie of all time?
Annie Hall.

What is your favourite romantic song?
'Into Your Arms' by Nick Cave.

What's your favourite Christmas song?
'Merry Christmas (War Is Over)' by Lennon.

What is your best ever Christmas present?
Snow.

And what is your worst?
One Christmas sock.

If you had to have sex with one British Prime Minister, who would it be?
Harold Macmillan? Stiff upper lip.

Who would you have as your naked stand-in?
Emmanuelle Beart – I think the similarities are obvious!!
Second choice the Pink Panther – ditto.

Is love actually all around?
Quite possibly it is – but none for me.

Love Questionnaire
Laura Linney (SARAH)

Who was the first person you ever loved – and how old were they and you?
George Harrison and I was six.

Who was the first person you loved in the movies?
My body fell in love with Errol Flynn and my heart fell in love with Gregory Peck.

What is your favourite romantic movie of all time?
Notorious.

What is your favourite romantic song?
'Come Fly With Me'.

What's your favourite Christmas song?
Music from the Vince Guaraldi Trio from *A Charlie Brown Christmas*
or 'Dahoo Doray' from *How the Grinch Stole Christmas / Horton Hears
A Hoo* by Dr Seuss.

What is your best ever Christmas present?
A prototype statue of Eleanor Roosevelt.

And what is your worst?
It's a toss-up between a really ugly painting of a cat and a McDonald's
gift certificate.

If you had to have sex with one British Prime Minister, who would it be?
Tony Blair – or Winston Churchill for the cred.

Who would you have as your naked stand-in?
The Swiss model Vendala to make the crew happy.

Is love actually all around?
Sometimes.

Love Questionnaire
Liam Neeson (DANIEL)

Who was the first person you ever loved – and how old were they and you?
The girl whose dad owned the Italian fish and chip shop in my town.
I guess I was ten – she would have been fifteen.

Who was the first person you loved in the movies?
Audie Murphy.

What is your favourite romantic movie of all time?
The Mummy (Boris Karloff's).

What is your favourite romantic song?
'Without You' by Harry Nilsson.

What's your favourite Christmas song?
'Fairy Tale Of New York' by Shane McGowan & Kirsty McColl.

What is your best ever Christmas present?
Socks and underpants (as an adult).

And what is your worst?
Socks and underpants (as a kid

If you had to have sex with one British Prime Minister, who would it be?
I guess Hugh Grant – but he'd better dress up as Natasha Richardson.

Who would you have as your naked stand-in?
Michelangelo's *God* – Sistine Chapel, Rome.

Is love actually all around?
We're all doomed.

Love Questionnaire
Lucia Moniz (AURELIA)

Who was the first person you ever loved – and how old were they and you?
Henry Thomas, Elliot in *E.T.* I was five years old when the movie came out.

What is your favourite romantic movie of all time?
E.T.

What is your favourite romantic song?
'Unforgettable'.

What is your favourite romantic poem?
'Ana Lucia' by Fernanda de Castro.

What's your favourite Christmas song?
'White Christmas'.

What is your best ever Christmas present?
Guitar.

And what is your worst?
I was given the same yellow toaster two years in a row by the same person.

If you had to have sex with one British Prime Minister, who would it be?
None of them. I would run away first.

Who would you have as your naked stand in?
Meryl Streep.

Is love actually all around?
Yes – especially when I was working on this movie – and tears and laughs.

Love Questionnaire
Martin Freeman (JOHN)

Who was the first person you ever loved – and how old were they and you?
I really liked Odeill Harin when I was five. Not sure how she felt about me though. I suppose real stuff would be with Michaela when I was seventeen – she was sixteen.

Who was the first person you loved in the movies?
Robert Powell as Jesus of Nazareth was a bit of an eye opener. Again, I think I was five. From a 'fancying' point of view, I've always been a bit funny about Jane Fonda and Marilyn Monroe.

What is your favourite romantic movie of all time?
Maybe *Brief Encounter* or *A Matter Of Life and Death*. I really liked *As Good As It Gets* as well. *Nil By Mouth*?

What is your favourite romantic song?
Oh God – 'Joy Inside My Tears' by Stevie Wonder, 'For Emily, Wherever I May Find Her' by Simon & Garfunkel, 'Thoughts Of Hogy Jane' by Nick Drake, 'If I Should Die Tonight' by Marvin Gaye – just too many. Oh, and 'Emmie' by Laura Nyro. Hundreds, basically.

What's your favourite Christmas song?
Well, 'Once In Royal David's City' is a proper tune. My Mum always puts on Handel's 'Messiah' at Christmas, so that's a festive piece in my head. And 'Merry Christmas (War is Over)' by John and Yoko. It's a good time and the sentiment is not one of feeding snow to fucking reindeer. Those kinds of songs don't do it for me.

What is your best ever Christmas present?
The birth of the Christ child, which forever more meant that men's souls are sacred. Oh, and an X-Box.

And what is your worst?
I was bought a cow once, and had nowhere to put it. It was a dreadful idea.

If you had to have sex with one British Prime Minister, who would it be?
Oh, Lloyd George, no question.

Who would you have as your naked stand-in?
Oh, Lloyd George, no question.

Is love actually all around?
Yeah. But so is everything else. I'd like to think that love's winning.

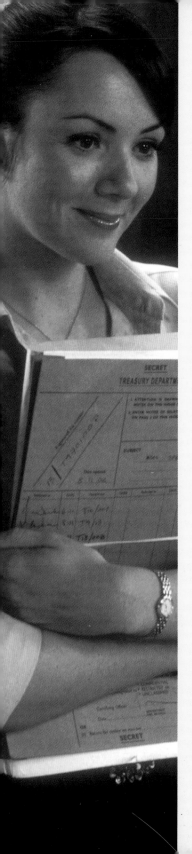

Love Questionnaire
Martine McCutcheon
(NATALIE)

Who was the first person you ever loved – and how old
were they and you?
My jazz teacher, David Samuel, when I was fifteen. He was
twenty-one or twenty-two and was gorgeous – all the girls
adored him. He eventually left and then rang my Mum to
ask me on a date when I was sixteen. We went to the
swimming baths but I was too scared to kiss him.

Who was the first person you loved in the movies?
I obviously have a thing for dancers – Patrick Swayze
(in *Dirty Dancing*) taught me how to dance. We did the lift
at the end, he told my Dad 'not to put Baby in the corner'.
Now I can Mumba, Cha Cha . . .

What is your favourite romantic movie of all time?
The Way We Were.

What is your favourite romantic song?
'Evergreen' by Barbra Streisand.

What's your favourite Christmas song?
'Last Christmas' by Wham.

What is your best ever Christmas present?
An ex-boyfriend standing naked with nothing but
a red ribbon tied on his privates.

And what is your worst?
An awful pair of gold lamé slippers my nan bought me
in true East End barmaid style. They had a leopard-skin
interior and I thought they were hideous.

If you had to have sex with one British Prime Minister,
who would it be?
Tony Blair.

Who would you have as your naked stand-in?
Penelope Cruz.

Is love actually all around?
No, but I wish it was.

Love Questionnaire
Rodrigo Santoro (KARL)

Who was the first person you ever loved – and how old were they and you?
My teacher – I was ten or eleven. She was a beautiful blonde and it was the
first time I realized I was going to be in trouble for the rest of my life.

What's your favourite Christmas song?
'All I Want For Christmas Is You'.

What is your best ever Christmas present?
A skateboard.

And what is your worst?
A pair of socks.

If you had to have sex with one British Prime Minister,
who would it be?
Pass.

Who would you have as your naked stand-in?
Rowan Atkinson.

Is love actually all around?
I totally believe it's all around, although some people can't
see it inside themselves. But it is there.

Some Strange Posters
Introduced by Richard Curtis

Designing the poster is one of the most delightful and frustrating parts of making a movie. In the back of your mind is the dream scenario where you come up with something like the perfect ones – *The Godfather*, *Jaws*, *The Graduate*. But it only happens about once every five years – so on the whole you just hope you don't end up with a turkey. I think we've done all right so far– there's one of the Bridget Jones posters I really like, the shot from above with Renée with her legs out, holding a glass of Chardonnay – and the *Notting Hill* one isn't bad – nice picture of Julia, though Hugh is a bit little and his face is a little pink. Here are some of the early stabs at posters for *Love Actually*. First, some of the ones we quite liked:

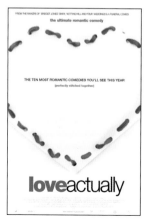

Next up, a hundred attempts to produce hearts in different ways – these are some of our favourites – the hands interestingly belong to Christy Turlington*.

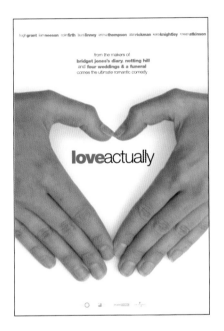

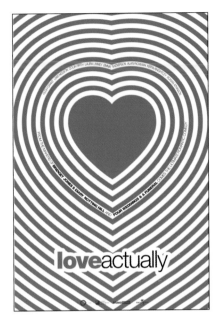

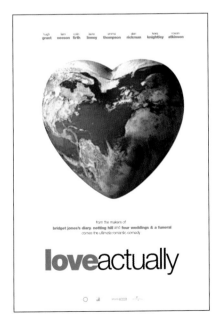

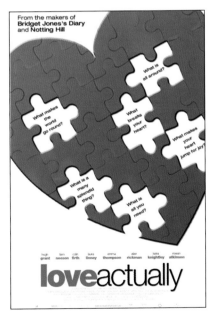

*That is a lie.

Then we told them to start getting a bit experimental . . .

 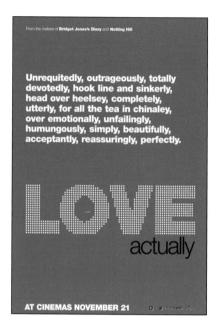

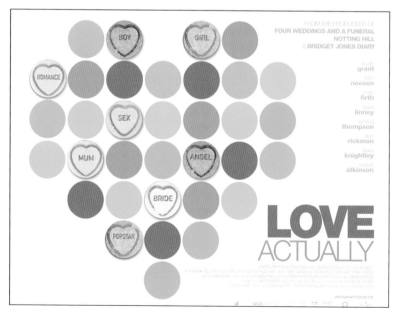

Then we told them to stop being so experimental . . .

Not before this bizarrre sequence – *Love Actually* as *Jurassic Park 4* . . .

And finally, over the page is either our favourite one of all, or the biggest marketing mistake a film could make. You can be the judge . . .

If you thought

NOTTING HILL
FOUR WEDDINGS AND A FUNERAL
and **BRIDGET JONES'S DIARY**

was a load of sentimental rubbish.

You're not going to like this.

loveactually

AT CINEMAS NOVEMBER 21

CAST IN ORDER OF APPEARANCE

Billy Mack	BILL NIGHY	US Expert	PETER MARINKER
Joe	GREGOR FISHER	Press Conference Reporters	KEIR CHARLES
Studio Engineer	RORY MacGREGOR		DORALY ROSEN
Jamie	COLIN FIRTH	PM's secretary	MEG WYNN OWEN
Jamie's girlfriend	SIENNA GUILLORY	Billy's Video Vixens	SARAH ATKINSON
Daniel	LIAM NEESON		CLARE BENNETT
Karen	EMMA THOMPSON		SARAH HOLLAND
Daisy	LULU POPPLEWELL		VICKI MURDOCH
Colin	KRIS MARSHALL		MEREDITH OSTROM
Mia	HEIKE MAKATSCH		KATHERINE POULTON
John	MARTIN FREEMAN		TUULI
Just Judy	JOANNA PAGE	As himself	MICHAEL PARKINSON
Peter	CHIWETEL EJIOFOR	Hospital patient	CIARAN O'DRISCOLL
Mark	ANDREW LINCOLN	Michael, Sarah's brother	MICHAEL FITZGERALD
Juliet	KEIRA KNIGHTLEY	Rufus, jewellery salesman	ROWAN ATKINSON
The Prime Minister	HUGH GRANT	Bernie, Karen's son	WILLIAM WADHAM
Annie	NINA SOSANYA	Language students	CATIA DUARTE
Terence, who's in charge	FRANK MOOREY		IGOR URDENKO
Pat the housekeeper	JILL FREUD		NAT UDOM
Natalie	MARTINE McCUTCHEON		INES BOUGHANMI
Sarah	LAURA LINNEY		YUK SIM YAU
The Wedding Singer	LYNDON DAVID HALL	Wisconsin taxi driver	JOHN SHARIAN
Jamie's bad brother	DAN FREDENBURGH	Barman	GLENN CONROY
Nancy the caterer	JULIA DAVIS	Stacey, American Dreamgirl	IVANA MILICEVIC
Tony	ABDUL SALIS	Jeannie, American Angel	JANUARY JONES
Funeral Priest	HELEN MURTON	Carol Anne, American Goddess	ELISHA CUTHBERT
Sam's Grandfather	EDWARD HARDWICKE	Record company executive	LAURA REES
Sam's Grandmother	CAROLINE JOHN	Jamie's sister	EMMA BUCKLEY
Sam	THOMAS SANGSTER	Jamie's mum	SHEILA ALLEN
Family Mourners	GEMMA ASTON	PM'S chauffeur, Terry	TERRY REECE
	MATT HARVEY	PM's bodyguard, Gavin	COLIN COULL
	ADRIAN PREATER	Harris Street old lady	MARGERY MASON
	JOANNA THAW	Harris Street little girl	KATHARINE BAILEY
Movie Director	ALAN BARNES	Her friends	TIFFANY BOYSELL
Movie Cameraman	SHAUGHAN SEYMOUR		GEORGIA FLINT
Wedding DJ	JUNIOR SIMPSON	Natalie's Mum	JOANNA BACON
Harry	ALAN RICKMAN	Natalie's Dad	BILL MOODY
Karl	RODRIGO SANTORO	Natalie's octopus brother, Keith	BILLY CAMPBELL
Radio Watford DJ1	BRIAN BOVELL	John's brother	PAUL SLACK
Radio Watford Receptionist	SARAH McDOUGALL	Mr Trench	ADAM GODLEY
Mike the DJ	MARCUS BRIGSTOCKE	Joanna Anderson	OLIVIA OLSON
Alex, Deputy Prime Minister	RICHARD HAWLEY	Mrs Jean Anderson	RUBY TURNER
Jeremy	WYLLIE LONGMORE	Backing-singer teacher	AMANDA GARWOOD
Cabinet Ministers	GILLIAN BARGE	Mr Anderson	ARTURO VENEGAS
	RICHARD WILLS-COTTON	Carol	CLAUDIA SCHIFFER
	KATE BOWES RENNA	Tommy, Carol's son	PATRICK DELANEY
	KATE GLOVER	Mr Barros	HELDER COSTA
	NICOLA McROY	Sophia Barros	CARLA VASCONCELOS
Ant	ANTHONY McPARTLIN	Airport Gate Man	STEWART HOWSON
Dec	DECLAN DONNELLY	Restaurant Proprietor	RAUL ATALAIA
Eléonore	ELIZABETH MARGONI	Harriet, the sexy one	SHANNON ELIZABETH
Aurelia	LUCIA MONIZ	Carla, the real friendly one	DENISE RICHARDS
The US President	BILLY BOB THORNTON		

UNIT LIST

Casting	Mary Selway CDG, Fiona Weir
Music Supervisor	Nick Angel
Music by	Craig Armstrong
Co-producers	Debra Heyward, Liza Chasin
Hair and Make-up Designer	Graham Johnston
Costume Designer	Joanna Johnston
Line Producer	Chris Thompson
Production Designer	Jim Clay
Director of Photography	Michael Coulter BSC
Editor	Nick Moore
Producers	Duncan Kenworthy,
	Tim Bevan, Eric Fellner
Writer/Director	Richard Curtis

Script Editor	Emma Freud
Production Manager	Tori Parry
First Assistant Director	Christopher Newman
Camera Operator	Peter Taylor
Script Supervisor	Lisa Vick
Production Sound Mixer	David Stephenson AMPS/CAS
Supervising Art Director	Jonathan McKinstry
Location Manager	Sue Quinn
Financial Controller	Michele Tandy
Post-Production Supervisor	Deborah Harding
Sound Supervisor	Glenn Freemantle
Music Editors	Michael Price
	Jon Olive AMPS

Chief Operating Officer	Angela Morrison
Executive in Charge of Production	Michelle Wright
Production Executive	Sarah-Jane Wright
Head of Legal & Business Affairs	Sheeraz Shah
Chief Financial Officer	Shefali Ghosh
Senior Legal & Business Affairs Executive	Gráinne McKenna
Legal & Business Affairs Executive	Lucy Wainwright
Executive Co-ordinator	Ann Lynch
Assistant Co-ordinator	Lucie Graves
Assistant to Tim Bevan	Callum Metcalfe
Assistant to Eric Fellner	Aliza James
Paralegal	Christina Angeloudes
Music Co-ordinator	Alexandra Hill

Production Co-ordinator	Simon Fraser
Assistant Production Co-ordinator	Una Hill
Second Assistant Director	Ben Howarth
Co-Second Assistant Director	Alexander Oakley
Third Assistant Director	Tom Glaisyer
Crowd Assistant Director	Susan Lawrence
Assistant to Duncan Kenworthy	Adam Tudhope
Assistants to Richard Curtis	Sarah McDougall, Clare Bennett
Assistant to Hugh Grant	Sara Woodhatch
Assistant to Liam Neeson	Manuela Cripps

Production Runner	James Bolton
.FT2 Continuity Trainee	Sheila Marshall
Floor Runners	Oliver Kersey
	Bryn Lawrence
	Jae Sung-Oh
Post-Production Runner	Sam Macrory

Focus Puller	Mik Allen
Clapper Loader	Oliver Loncraine
Grip	Richard Broome
Steadicam Operator	Paul Edwards

Video Assist	Stephen Lee
Assistant Video Operator	Rory Fry
Camera Trainee	Luke Coulter
Sound Maintenance	Colin Wood
Sound Assistant	Amie Stephenson

First Assistant Accountant	Penny Powell
Assistant Accountants	James Richardson
	Fran Triefus
PG Asst. Trainee Accountant	Chris Norman

Location Unit Managers	Joseph Jayawardena
	Jonathan Hook
Assistant Location Manager	Aurelia Thomas
Location Assistant	Lucy Foulds

Casting Assistant	Sophie Shand
Children's Casting	Shaheen Baig
Casting of Joanna	Stephanie Corsalini
Portuguese Casting	Camilla-Valentine Isola

Documentary Kissing Footage Cameraman	Mike Eley
2nd Unit Cameraman	David Morgan
Additional 2nd Unit Cameraman	Mike Brewster
'B' Camera Operators	Martin Hume
	John Palmer
'B' Camera Focus Puller	James Bloom
Crane Grip	Andy Friswell
Sound Playback	Mike Harris

First Assistant Editor	Peter Dansie
Avid Assistant Editor	Tania Clarke
Second Assistant Editor	Deborah Richardson
Conforming Editors	Paul Clegg, Martin Corbett,
	Daryl Jordan, Julian May,
	Ben Renton, Christian Wheeler
NFTS Trainee	Peter Lambert

Make-Up Artists	Lorna McGowan
	Kate Benton

Assistant Costume Designers	Marlene Lawlor
	Samantha Heskia
Costume Supervisor	Mark Ferguson
Set Supervisor	Amanda Trewin
Set Costumiers	Martin Chitty
	Leigh Nicol
Costume Assistants	Charlotte Finlay,
	Charlotte Sewell, Jo Roderick,
	Lisa Bracey, Frank Gallacher
Costume Department Runner	Magdalena Natalia Witko

Art Directors	Rod McLean
	Justin Warburton-Brown
Stand-by Art Director	Ashley Winter
Storyboard Artist	Jane Clark
Assistant Art Director	Heidi Gibb
Draughtsmen	Roger Bowles
	Philip Harvey
	Jonathan Houdling
	Emma Vane
Junior Draughtsman	Antonio Calvo-Dominguez
Graphic Designer	Jools Faiers
Art Department Assistants	Oliver Goodier
	Andrea Couch
Art Department Runner	Helen Chapman

'Christmas Uncovered'
Exhibition Photographs by David Bellemère
Set Decorator Caroline Smith
Assistant Set Decorator Sophie Newman
Drapes Master Chris Seddon

Production Buyer Dave Morris
Props Master Barry Gibbs
Prop Storeman Darryl Paterson
Chargehand Dressers Roy Chapman
Kevin Wheeler
Dressing Props John Botton
Colin Ellis
Jason Hopperton

Chargehand Standby Propman Bradley Torbett
Standby Propman Jason Torbett
FT2 Props Trainee Esta Morris

Construction Manager Stephen Bohan
Assistant Construction Manager Seamus O'Sullivan
Construction Buyer Zoë Robertson
Supervising Carpenters David Lowery
Tom Martin
Eamon McLoughlin
Danny O'Regan
Chargehand Carpenters Peter Browne
Martin Freeman
John O'Brien
Dave Youngs
Stand-by Carpenter John McGee

Carpenters Joseph Alley, David Barker,
Lee Biggs, James Buxton,
Eamonn Cann, Robert Cann,
Paul Carpenter, Bernie Collins,
Peter Collins, Nigel Crafts,
Derek Dawson, Lee Edwards,
David Gibson, Andy Good,
Nick Goodall, Gavin Gordon,
Peter Grove, Kevin Harris,
Tom Hayes, Gary Hedges,
Barnaby Inman, Anthony
McGee, Nicholas Lloyd,
Stephen McGregor, Stephen
Murray, Peter Nodwell, Geoff
Nolan, Barry O'Brien, Colin
Osgood, Jason Phelps, David
Philpott, Russell Sargent,
Richard Shackleton, Rolf
Snellgrove, Paul Waterman,
Paul Webb, Matthew Whelan,
Mark Wilkinson

Trainee Carpenters Mark Weston
Roy O'Brien
Chargehand Wood Machinist Stephen Weston
Wood Machinist David Allistone

H.O.D. Painter Gary Crosby
Supervising Painter Dean Dunham
Chargehand Painters David Haberfield
Albert Roper
Steve Williamson
Clive Ward
Stand-by Painter Brian Morris

Painters Perry Bell, Frank Berlin,
Ben Crosby, Fred Crosby,
Mark Dowling, Trevor Eve,
Michael Finlay, Craig Gleeson,
Alan Grenham, Jesse Hammond,
John Hersey, Garry Higgins,
Gary Lowe, Charles McGinlay,
John McGuigan, Glenn Start,
Jeff Sullivan, Kenneth Welland,
Ian Zawadzki

Painters' Labourers Peter Kane
David Lainsbury
Ian Tansey
Trainee Painters Adam Crosby
Luke Goodman
Chargehand Sprayer John Butler

H.O.D. Plasterer Richard McCarthy
Supervising Plasterer Adrian Aitken
Chargehand Plasterer Cliff Etheridge

Plasterers Nick Barringer, Ian Burrows,
Robert Byron, Delmont
Earwicker, Stephen Fountain,
Geoffrey Grant, Nigel
Henderson, Sean Higgins,
Thomas Mangan, Peter
McCarroll, Stephen Morris,
Stephen Page, Steven
Ponting, Steve Tranfield, Ettore
Venturini, Darrell Williams,
Eddie Wolstencroft

Plasterers' Labourers Gary Burns
Mark Williams

H.O.D. Rigger Peter Hawkins
Chargehand Rigger Frederick Crawford
Supervising Rigger Ronald Meeks
Stand-by Rigger David Weller

Riggers Stephen Dunn, Martin Goddard,
Martin Hawkins, Lee Jones,
Colin Smith

H.O.D. Stagehand Derek Whorlow
Supervising Stagehand George King
Stand-by Stagehand Mark Goodman

Stagehands Peter Browne, Stephen
Dunsford, Robert Flint,
Michael Webb, Keith Weston

Gaffer Terry Edland
Best Boy Wayne Leach

Electricians Mark Evans, Warren Evans,
Patrick O'Flynn,, David Sinfield,
Karl Thomas

Generator Operator Mark Laidlaw
Practical Electrician Darren Gatrell
Practical Electrician for
Construction/Art Department Joe McGee
Rigging Gaffer Tony Hayes

The British Crew

Studio Chargehand Rigging Electrician	Tom Brown
Rigging Electricians	Kenneth Monger, Kevin Edland
Specialist Lighting Electrician	Chris Craig
H.O.D. Electrical Rigger	William Beenham
Electrical Riggers	Gary Dormer, Paul Harford, Scott Hillier, William Howe
Special Effects Supervisor	Richard Conway
Special Effects Technicians	Sam Conway
	Mark White
Stunt Co-ordinator	Lee Sheward
Stunt Double for Aurelia	Tracey Caudle
Stunt Doubles for Sam	Talila Craig, Avril Soards
Choreographer	Jonathan Lunn
Unit Publicist	Sarah Clark
Stills Photographer	Peter Mountain
Mark's Wedding Video and 'Behind the Scenes' Footage	Jonathan Richardson
Utility Stand-Ins	James Chasey
	Georgie Sayer
Health & Safety Officer	James Blackwell
Unit Nurse	Pat Barr
Construction Nurses	Ruth Nicol
	Carrie Johnson
Tutors	Matthew J. Hogden
	Charles Howes
Transport Captain	Roy Clarke
Unit Drivers	Mike Beaven, Miklos Kozma, Terry Reece, John Smith, Tony Wadsworth
Driver to Duncan Kenworthy'	Enyo Mortty
Driver to Richard Curtis	Simon Hudnott
Driver to Hugh Grant	Peter Devlin
Driver to Liam Neeson'	Simon Saunders
Minibus Drivers	Mike Moran
	John Burden
Location Vehicle Drivers	George Corrigan, Keith Ellis, Mark Hatchell, Tommy Hunt, Tom Innes, Townley Knott, Martin Lewis, Martin Parry, George Yeung
Facilities Supervisor	Albert Smith
Facility Drivers	Mark Allen
	Andy Carter
	Barry Stone

FRENCH UNIT

Production Service Company	Bay Vista Production Services
	Antoine Sabarros
Production Manager	Raphaël Benoliel
Assistant Director	Gilles Kenny
Production Co-ordinator	Laurence Coutaud-Garnier
Assistant Production Co-ordinator	Emmanuelle Breuil
Office Runner	Jennifer Simonnet
Accountant	Isabelle Lippitsch

Location Manager	Arnaud Duterque
Assistant Location Managers	Gerard Hubert
	Olivier Coquillon
	David Piechaszeck
Extras Casting Director	Samia Fadli
Prop Buyer	Jean-Paul Bernardi
Construction	Jean Preiss
Gaffer	Patrick Allard
Transport Captain	Matthieu Rubin
Craft Service	Stephane Santinelli
	Nicolas Sabarros
Dialogue/ADR Editor	Gillian Dodders
Effects Editor	Mark Heslop
Foley Editor	Graham Peters
Assistant Sound Editors	Andy Wilkinson
	Tom Sayers
	Susan French
Re-recording Mixers	Robin O'Donoghue
	Richard Street
	Graham Daniel
Assisted by	Nigel Bennett, Adam Daniel
Sound Re-recordist	Esther Smith
ADR Mixer	Aad Wirtz at Interact Sound
Foley Mixer	Kevin Tayler
Foley Artists	Felicity Cotterell
	Lionel Selwyn
Crowd Voices	Sync or Swim
ADR voice casting	Jay Benedict and
	Phoebe Scholfield
Preview Re-recording Mixer	Brendan Nicholson
Sound Re-recorded at	Shepperton Studios, Shepperton, England
Visual Effects & Digital Grading by	Framestore CFC London
Visual Effects Supervisor	Tim Webber
Visual Effects Producer	Tim Keene
Visual Effects Compositors	Christian Manz, Nick Seal
Digital Grading Producer	Claire McGrane
Digital Grading Colourists	Adam Inglis, Asa Shoul
Digital Conform	Steve Wagendorp
Digital Lab	Andy Burrows, Maria Stroka
Visual Effects Editorial	Roz Lowrie
Main Title and End Sequence Design by	Momoco/Maguffin
Camera & Lenses Supplied by	One8Six Ltd
Lighting Equipment by	Lee Lighting
Louma Crane	Louma UK
Louma Technician	Adam Samuelson
Graphics, Computer & Video Playback	Compuhire
Editing Equipment	Hyperactive Broadcast Ltd
Sound Post-Production by	Reelsound Ltd
Digital Projection Equipment	Bell Theatre Services
Cherrypickers Supplied by	Nationwide Access Ltd
Additional Generators	Powerent
Trucks and Facilites	Cavalier International Transport
	Lays International
	Location Facilities
	Willies Wheels

Low Loader	Bickers Action
Prop Vehicles	Action Cars
Color by	Deluxe
Laboratory Contact	Clive Noakes
Colour Timer	Dave Rees
Negative Cutting	Cutting Edge
End Roller Digital Compositing by	Cineimage
Dolby Sound Consultant	Nick Watson
Security	Lew Morgan
Background Artists Supplied by	The Casting Collective
	2020 Casting
Costumiers	Academy Costume
	Carlo Manzi Rentals
Catering Supplied by	AVC Catering
Crowd Catering	Fayre Do's
Caterers	Sophie Aitken, Mitchell Brown,
	Vince Jordan, Tricia O'Connor,
	Clive Putman
Telecine	Midnight Transfer
Insurance provided by	Aon/Albert G Ruben
Legal Services	Christine Somerville
	Patricia Mary Murphy
Legal Clearances	Marshall/Plumb Research
	Associates, Inc.
Clearance & Product	
Placement Coordinators	Bellwood Media Ltd
Clearance Co-ordinator	Eth Ibrahim-Flint

Music Consultant	Kirsten Lane-Right Music Ltd
Post-Production Accountants	Post Sums Ltd
Post-Production Scripts	Sapex Scripts
Post-Production Consultancy	Steve Harrow, Steeple Post-
	Production Services Ltd
Executive in Charge of Film Music	Kathy Nelson
for Universal Studios	
Score Composed, Produced	
and Arranged by	Craig Armstrong
Recorded and Mixed by	Geoff Foster at Air Studios,
	London
Assistant Engineers	Jake Jackson, Chris Barrett
	and Olga Fitzroy
Orchestrations by	Craig Armstrong and
	Matt Dunkley
Orchestra Contractor	Isobel Griffiths
Orchestra Leaders	Gavyn Wright and Perry
	Montague-Mason
Piano by	Simon Chamberlain
	and Craig Armstrong
Guitar by	Craig Armstrong
Solo Clarinet by	Matthew Hunt
Gospel Choir	Metro Voices
Choirmaster	Jenny O'Grady
Music Conducted by	Cecilia Weston
North Studio Engineer and	
additional programming	David Donaldson
Assistant to Craig Armstrong	Emma Ford
US Music Consultant	Jeffrey Pollack

The French Crew

And Finally ...

Just for the scrapbook – a couple of last extra things. First, some of the curiously similar logos for *Love Actually* from around the world.

simplesmente**amor**
(loveactually)
BRAZIL

realmente**amor**
LATIN AMERICAN SPANISH

loveactually
l'amore davvero
ITALY

Tatsächlich...**Liebe**
GERMANY

ラブ・アクチュアリー
JAPAN

o **amor**acontece
PORTUGAL

愛是您愛是我
TAIWAN

אהבה
זה כל הסיפור
ISRAEL

러브 액츄얼리
KOREA

Well, not always 'Love Actually'. In Taiwan the film is called *Love Is You, Love Is Me* because there isn't actually a word for 'actually' in Taiwan. But others have experienced stranger things – in Italy *Bridget Jones's Diary* was called *Bridget Jones – Chocolate for Breakfast*.

And last of all, just for the record, the call sheet for the day of the filming of the final scene in Heathrow Airport. It was a big day ...